In All Things

Religious Faith and American Culture

Papers of the Inaugural Conference of
The Jesuit Institute at Boston College

edited by
Robert J. Daly, S.J.

Sheed & Ward

Sheed & Ward™ is a service of National Catholic Reporter Publishing Company, Inc.

Library of Congress Catalog Card Number: 89-64479

ISBN: 1-55612-315-9

Published by: Sheed & Ward
               115 E. Armour Blvd. P.O. Box 419492
               Kansas City, MO 64141

To order, call: (800) 333-7373

Contents

Culture and Belief

Foreword

As in many other Jesuit universities, especially in the U.S., the Jesuits at Boston College have recently been engaged in intensive discussions about the Catholic and Jesuit character of their institution. In the recent past, most Catholic colleges and universities have experienced rapid transformations from strongly denominational schools, governed largely as extensions of their founding religious groups, into modern institutions comfortably taking their place in the mainstream of American higher education. As is already the established pattern in American private higher education, will these changes lead to a dilution of religious ethos? And, in any case, what is the role the founding religious community, now a small numerical minority, should continue to play in these institutions?

At Boston College, one of the most visible results of the effort to meet the challenges contained in such questions has been the founding of the Jesuit Institute.

The idea of the Jesuit Institute grew out of discussions within the Jesuit Community, which then effectively founded the Institute with a generous endowment in 1987. Formally constituted in 1988 as a university research institute, this new venture is designed to help strengthen the Catholic and Jesuit character of Boston College by supporting research across the disciplines of the university.

The task of fleshing out the plan was committed to a director and advisory board. Beginning in December, 1987, this group, men and women, Jesuits and laypersons, quickly evolved into a planning and working committee receptive to the faith-inspired gesture of the founding Jesuit Community, and sensitive to the hope-inspired vision of Jesuits and others for the future of Boston College. As they took up the task of charting the course and shaping the vision, some fundamental principles gradually fell into place:

1. Research, especially interdisciplinary, will be the Institute's primary activity.

2. The Institute will be committed both to the highest quality of research and to its publication.

3. The Institute will not establish new academic programs. It will attempt to encourage rather than absorb or seek control over existing programs or program elements already consonant with its goals.

4. The Institute will seek to identify and support reflection and research on issues and concerns which should be part of the research profile of a Catholic university, but which, for whatever reason, do not receive the attention they merit.

5. The Institute will focus on questions and issues which are located at the intersection of faith and culture, which affect or are affected by religious knowledge or faith experience.

6. The Institute is committed to pursue its goals by the means appropriate to a funded research institute, i.e., by sponsoring and funding—possibly also in conjunction with other funding agencies—research scholars, research projects, conferences, lectures, seminars, consultations, etc.

While these principles were emerging, planning for the Institute's Inaugural Conference was also moving ahead. This conference was not merely to publicize the Institute, but also to advance the practical task of clarifying its specific goals and strategies.

At the same time, the advisory board continued its search for overarching themes by which to channel the Institute's still relatively modest resources. The "intersection" metaphor mentioned above in the fifth principle quickly became a key concept in these efforts, providing the overarching theme for the first research grants awarded for academic year 1989-1990: "Religious Faith and the Searches for Knowledge." This theme was further specified for the 1990-1991 grant period in order to welcome proposals specifically from scholars in the natural sciences and the social sciences.

In the months leading up to the Inaugural Conference, at a time when the first issues of the Jesuit Institute *Newsletter* were being distributed, the Institute director met in small groups with some 330 colleagues from the university community. In all these meetings, the agenda was the same: providing information about the new Institute, clarifying its nature and role in the University, seeking feedback and suggestions.

These meetings, spaced over five months, contributed immensely to increased clarity about the goals and purposes and some of the specific challenges of the Institute. Among these challenges is the increasingly obvious need to develop appropriate ways to affirm that, in being committed to help Boston College become more Jesuit and Catholic, the Jesuit Institute is committed to do this in a manner that is consistent with the nature and processes of a modern university. In the past two centuries, Roman Catholicism resisted some of the key developments of modernity, especially in the natural and social sciences. For many, this part of our Catholic heritage leaves a strong note of ambiguity about the relationship of a modern research university to the life of Roman Catholicism. However, as the discussions accompanying the establishment of the Jesuit Institute at Boston College have brought out, some very positive elements have also come from our heritage.

First, there seems to be a felicitously symbiotic relationship between a fundamental Jesuit charism and the true spirit of academic research. In the culminating exercise of his *Spiritual Exercises*, the

Contemplation for obtaining Divine Love, St. Ignatius encourages Jesuits and all who make the Exercises to see all things as being from God and of God. The specifically academic way of living out this Ignatian charism of finding or seeing God in all things is the attitude of intellectual openness. This attitude motivates the scholar to be radically open to all knowledge and strongly supportive of research in all areas of academic activity. It is the obvious inspiration for the title of the Institute's first major publication: *In All Things.*

Second, there is a close affinity between the central principle of selection for Jesuit Institute-sponsored research and the Ignatian criteria for the selection of ministries. Ignatius wanted Jesuits to be ready to travel to any part of the world and undertake whatever the church most needed to have done at that time. This principle expressed in the Jesuit motto, *Ad Majorem Dei Gloriam* (For the Greater Glory of God), is at the heart of what the Jesuit Institute has come to recognize as its primary function: to identify and support that kind of authentic research which should characterize a university that is Jesuit and Catholic.

It was in the context of these reflections and developments that the speakers of the Inaugural Conference prepared their remarks and then the more extensively developed papers which appear in this volume. How remarkably well they did this is evidenced in the following pages. The fact that this specific context did not lessen but notably enhanced the general relevance of these papers as significant studies in their own right seems to suggest initial confirmation that the Jesuit Institute is well launched.

The Papers

The Inaugural Conference ran from 4 pm, Friday, April 21 to 5 pm, Saturday, April 22, 1989. John W. Padberg, S.J., presented the opening, keynote address by speaking directly to the opportunities and challenges opened up by the founding of the Jesuit Institute at Boston College. The other speakers spoke not directly to the Institute but to a range of concrete issues chosen both for their importance in themselves and for their anticipated relevance to the work of the Jesuit Institute. They were arranged in three panels.

First, Jean Bethke Elshtain, Preston N. Williams and Richard A. McCormick, S.J., addressed a broad, complex range of issues under the perenially critical themes of "Family, Culture, and Ethics."

Second, John W. O'Malley, S.J., Anne E. Patrick, S.N.J.M., and Denis Donoghue addressed the theme: "Interrelating Religion and the Arts." This theme is illustrative of how the Jesuit Institute envisions its role in general and at Boston College in particular. In contrast to the European Church from which it largely grew, the North American Catholic Church, shaped by its immigrant and working-class past, has yet to develop strong ties to the arts. Boston College, along with most Roman Catholic educational institutions in the U.S., must now face this challenge.

Third, Rosemary Haughton, John A. Coleman, S.J., and Michael J. Buckley, S.J., under the theme of "Culture and Belief," began a critical exploration of some of the challenging (and often neglected) issues that arise at the intersections of faith and reason, culture and belief.

In the conference panel format, the remarks of each speaker were relatively brief. After the conference, the speakers carefully prepared a significantly expanded version of their remarks for publication in this volume.

Robert J. Daly, S.J.
Director
The Jesuit Institute at Boston College

Imagining a Heritage: The Jesuit Institute

John W. Padberg, S.J.
The Institute of Jesuit Sources, St. Louis, MO

The founding of the Jesuit Institute is an extraordinary event. It looks forward to the future and back to a heritage. The year of its founding has at least the potentiality of ranking as an imaginative venture with the years of four other such ventures, 1540, 1547, 1583 and 1789. It will depend on how well, how vigorously the quality of imagination which infused the events which then took place and which, it seems to me, has brought the Jesuit Institute into being, will continue to infuse, inspire, pervade the Institute now and in the years to come. It is that topic of imagining a heritage at the Jesuit Institute which I wish to address this afternoon.

Before I do so, however, let me first, on behalf of all of us here, congratulate and thank all those who have brought into being our present happy occasion and the Institute itself. May I mention specifically Father Robert Daly, the Director of the Institute, its advisory board which has worked so long and so diligently, the hundreds of members of Boston College who have contributed in countless meetings their insights to the nature and goals of the Institute, Boston College itself and Father J. Donald Monan, S.J., its president, in their generosity, and, most importantly, the members of the Jesuit community at Boston College, especially Father Joseph Duffy, S.J., the rector at the very beginning of the Institute and Father William Barry, S.J., the present rector. That community has had the imagination and the courage and the generosity to propose and to venture upon this new manner of expressing the Jesuit charism.

1

Let me return now to those four dates mentioned a moment ago, 1540, 1547, 1583 and 1789. They mark events in the history of the Society of Jesus and I want to recall them for the sake of the Jesuit Institute itself so that it might experience in its corporate personality what Thomas Fuller recounted as the benefits of history for us individual persons: "History maketh a young man to be old without either wrinkles or gray hair; privileging him with the experience of age without either the infirmities or inconveniences thereof."[1] Most importantly, it was the willingness to imagine previously unexplored possibilities which brought about those events and then carried them far beyond their simple beginnings.

In the first part of these remarks, I want to say something about what happened at each of those dates. In the second part, I want to suggest that the enduring principles and the heritage which animated those four events ought to animate the Jesuit Institute, too, for the future.

In 1539, 450 years ago this year, Ignatius Loyola and nine companions sat down to deliberate in common on how they would both maintain together their friendship in the Lord and go out separately to do the work of the Lord in lands as widely distant as Italy and the Indies. The results of their deliberations, approved by the Church in 1540, was the establishment of the Society of Jesus.[2] We do not recognize today how very unusual this new religious order was in the Church because so many of its features became, especially from the nineteenth century on, common to many religious congregations. The Society of Jesus was an imaginative response to the spirit of the times and the needs of the Church. It was utterly mobile, without the constraints of cloister or of the chanting of the official prayer of the Church, able to go anywhere for the preaching of the Gospel, not reliant on the deliberation of a community chapter but upon the intimate personal knowledge of member and superior, at the immediate service of the Pope in order to be sent where he thought its members might best serve the Lord, selective in recruitment, respectful of all serious learning and eager to make use of it, including such use in the unusually lengthy training of its members, imbued with the experience of the Spiritual Exercises common to all its members, seeing all of creation as a good gift of God and willing to employ all creatures in the praise and service of God.[3] The Society had also many of the characteristics of the older religious orders, but no one had ever before combined the older characteristics and these new insights. Ignatius Loyola had the imagination to do so; he had the colleagues who could grasp what he was trying to do; he had the organizational skills to bring together effectively that imagination and those colleagues in the Society of Jesus. Within twenty years, the Jesuits were everywhere from Ethiopia to Poland, from Sicily to Brazil, in every conceivable kind of work, yet bound together by a common spirit and a common ideal. We may take the Society of Jesus for granted today, praise it or blame it (and there are enough people who would vigorously do either of these), admire or be puzzled by it, but the creation of the Jesuits was an extraordinary act of imagination, organization and colleagueship (the first Jesuits called themselves "friends in the Lord"); and in its results, it went far beyond what anyone might have conceived at its founding.

The Society was officially approved and began its existence in 1540, but between that year and 1547, the second of our dates, there was no such thing as a Jesuit school explicitly for laypeople.

Gradually, through experience, the early Society saw the advantages of schools and then, in 1547, the Spanish viceroy of Sicily requested that a college be set up in Messina. Why? For the reform of the island of Sicily, he said. That college was the first school set up by the Society of Jesus directly for lay students. Ignatius, in sending ten of his colleagues there, ten of the very best men he had in what was still a very small Society, told them as they left Rome for Messina, "If we live for ten years, we shall see great things in the Society of Jesus." Indeed they did! At the end of ten years, by 1556, the year Ignatius died, there were 40 colleges spread throughout Europe and already in parts of the New World, in India and a few places in Africa. From the beginning, they regarded organization of the school and of the curriculum as important, and so great was the need for such an organized system of education and so great its desirability that the Jesuits were besieged with requests to start institutions everywhere throughout Europe and in mission lands. We take such an organized and institutionalized system for granted. But it took a great leap of the imagination to bring it into existence.

They were also at times urged to become members of the faculty or administration of already-existing institutions, which were not specifically Jesuit. At this point I would like to pause and tell you a story which may (I do not say necessarily will) give you some vivid sense that Boston College itself is indeed in the great tradition of Jesuit education. It is a story about the experiences of the first Jesuit to be rector or president of a university. His name was Peter Canisius, now St. Peter Canisius, and he was elected by the faculty to that office at the University of Ingolstadt, today the University of Munich, in October, 1550, 439 years ago. In a letter to Ignatius Loyola in Rome a few weeks later, he told him what in practice the office of president involved:

> Governing this place is bringing me a good deal of trouble and precious little so far in the way of obvious results. The rector's [for our purposes, read "president's"] principal duties are to enroll new students, to force debtors to pay their bills, to listen to the complaints which men and women citizens of the town bring against the young men, to arrest, reprimand and jail the students who get drunk and roam around the streets at night, and finally to preside at official festivities and at academic functions connected with the conferral of degrees . . . . They say, and it's true, that the lawyers run the place.

Have things really changed so much over the centuries?

Let me return now to what happened in the foundation of those Jesuit schools originally started in 1547. Within 50 years, by 1600, there were 245 Jesuit schools around the world. By 1740, 200 years after the founding of the Society, there were 700 schools for lay students and 175 seminaries and houses of study for those preparing for the priesthood, all run by the Society of Jesus. Those schools were all based in their operations on that famous manual of procedure, the *Ratio Studiorum*, which was mostly a handbook of specific teaching methods set out with admirable clarity for the classes of the day. One of the editions of the *Ratio*, however, had as its preface a general essay by a famous Spanish Jesuit educator named Ledesma in which he set forth a statement of the purposes which the Society of Jesus had in conducting schools and universities. Let me quote directly what Ledesma, set down as that Jesuit purpose. The Society was to run schools, first, because they supply men with many advantages for practical living; secondly, "because they contribute to the right government of public affairs and to the proper making of laws; third, because they give ornament, splendor and perfection to the rational nature of man; and fourth, and what is most important, because they are the bulwark of religion and guide man most surely and easily to the achievement of his last end."[4] Now of course, it did not always work out in practice that way, and another early Jesuit, Pedro Ribadeneyra, even while defending Jesuit education, had to admit that a lot of people contended that "it is a repulsive, annoying and burdensome thing to guide and teach and try to control a crowd of young people, who are naturally so frivolous, so restless, so talkative and so unwilling to work that even their parents cannot keep them at home. So it happens that our young Jesuits, who are involved in teaching them, lead a very strained life, wear down their energies and damage their health."[5]

Let us return now for a few more minutes to history. We left the Society of Jesus in 1740 with 700 schools. By 1773, they were all destroyed when the Church suppressed the Jesuits at the insistence of and, indeed, under threats of schism in the Church from the Bourbon monarchies of France, Spain and Naples, aided by Portugal. Sixteen years later, the French Revolution came along with all of the institutional, social, psychological and religious havoc which the revolution caused to Church, society and states throughout Europe. At the time that the French Revolution was coming to an end, the Society of Jesus, partly restored in the earlier turmoil of the 1800s, had 12 small, struggling schools. Four were in

Italy, two in France, five, surprisingly, in Russia, and one, equally surprisingly, in the United States. But the story of that imaginative American venture and its consequences will wait for 1789, the fourth of the dates which I mentioned earlier.

Let me go back now to the third date, 1583. A little more than 400 years ago, a thirty-year-old Jesuit priest, Matteo Ricci, set foot on the mainland of China. His work? In the long run, quite simply to bring Christianity to China. How? By trying to put into effect the principles elaborated by one of the greatest and most farseeing proponents of inculturation who has ever lived, Alessandro Valignano. Valignano, an Italian like Ricci, was, at the still early age of 34, delegate of the General of the Society of Jesus to all of the lands of the Far East where the Jesuits were working or might work. Through tireless journeys from India through Indonesia to China to Japan and back and forwards again for better than 30 years, he developed, far in advance of his time, almost all of the principles which we today take for granted, at least in theory if not that very often in practice, of how one civilization or culture should best meet another if it comes not as conqueror but as friend and eventual colleague.[6]

Let me describe those principles briefly. They were, first, a sympathy and a respect for the cultural, social, intellectual, and spiritual values of the people among whom one was working; secondly, a perfect command of the language, the idiom, in which that civilization or culture was incarnated; third, science and scholarship in the service of introducing the values and ethos of one civilization or culture to another, quite frankly in this case in the service of introducing the Christian faith to China; fourth, a long-term endeavor of serious writing and personal dialogue; fifth, concern for the groups upon whom a society depended for its leadership and cohesion, especially, in his time, the scholarly communities and government officials; and, finally, the supreme importance of the example of one's personal values lived out in one's life.

Ricci was to spend a lifetime wholeheartedly incarnating all of those principles of Valignano. He lived, studied, spoke and indeed thought in the language and the manners and the idioms of China. Twenty major works in Chinese itself on mathematics, astronomy, literature and apologetics came from his pen, among which rank some of the classics of Chinese literature.

Most importantly, Ricci had the imagination to see that Christianity could be truly compatible with a non-European culture, and need not simply be presented in its sixteenth-century Western European garb. He had the extraordinary ability to see how this might be true, not only in theory but also in practice. That meant especially the determination to understand sympathetically the central facets of Chinese civilization and to begin to make of them a synthesis with Christianity which would be true both to that civilization and to the faith. Just as important was Ricci's determination to find contemporary Chinese expressions for the timeless truths of Christianity. This was really the first such endeavor, methodically and seriously undertaken in the context of a fully developed and immensely sophisticated civilization, since better than 1500 years before. In that sole previous example, the Hebraic experience and expression of revelation had been transmuted into the vocabulary of Greece and Rome, out of the experience and reflection of the new converts of the Roman empire to the infant Christian Church.

In this extraordinary work of imaginative adaptation, in a totally different culture, for better than a quarter of a century, Ricci built up institutional support and had the colleagueship of his brethren in the Society of Jesus. By no means did every individual, even among his fellow Jesuits, agree with him and his methods. When did all Jesuits *ever* agree on anything? But he did have the support of the Society as an institution, and this kind of support immensely multiplied the fruits of his labors. Ironically, a century and a half later, the Church, another institution, with its structures and its imagination lodged in Europe, could not recognize what was happening as the Church in China attempted to become truly Chinese without being any the less universal. It was that failure of imagination and that institutional intransigence which brought down into ruins the whole effort of the Chinese mission. James Billington, the Librarian of Congress, recently called the Jesuit Chinese project in its denouement an heroic, tragic enterprise. He then briefly noted its contrast with another heroic and so far successful enterprise, the Jesuit system of higher education in the United States. And that brings us to the fourth of our dates, 1789.

In 1789, a little more than two centuries after the Society of Jesus entered China, it began its work of education in the United States. This year we celebrate the two-hundredth anniversary of Jesuit education in this country. It began with the foundation of a school at Georgetown in 1789. This is the fourth imaginative venture and heritage upon which the Jesuit Institute might well draw for its future.

Remember, at the time of the independence of this country, Roman Catholics were a small and suspect minority, 30,000 people out of three million, about 1% of the population. They were regarded by most of their Protestant neighbors, quite frankly, as members of a church called regularly in some of the New England public school books used then and through the 19th century "the whore of Babylon" and "the harlot of Rome." The Church was defensive, and understandably so. And yet John Carroll could see the need for a well-educated laity and clergy in the American Church, still in its infancy but destined to grow even beyond his generous imagination. So embracing was that imagination, too, that he could say in the initial prospectus for his institution that "agreeably to the liberal principle of our Constitution, the [school] will be open to students of every religious profession" (Inaugural Prospectus, 1786).

No one would then have ventured to predict that starting with that single small academy on the Potomac, the Catholic higher education system in the United States would have come into being. Yet today there are more than 250 such Catholic colleges and universities, 28 of them Jesuit, spread from places such as Boston College and Holy Cross in the East to Spring Hill and Loyola-New Orleans in the South, to St. Louis and Marquette and John Carroll in the Midwest, to the University of San Francisco and Seattle and Loyola in the West. Twenty-three of those schools came into existence between 1814 and 1914, one new college or university almost every four years. And then in the next 50 years, to 1964, five more schools were founded. By that time, in addition to the current 28 Jesuit colleges and universities, there were almost 50 high schools which the Jesuits also staffed. This extraordinary flowering of Jesuit educational institutions would not have been possible without the imagination of their founders, people, for instance, such as Father McElroy, the founder of Boston College, or rather Father Gasson, its "second founder" here at the Heights. Those schools would not have existed to our own day without the commitment and insight and increasing collaboration of Jesuits and of lay men and women. They would not have met the vicissitudes of two centuries and be flourishing today without a continued effort at imaging how best to respond to the changing needs and opportunities of the United States of which they are a part. For an example, look only at Boston College and recall how very different this institution is today from 50 or 20 or even 10 years ago and how, still, it remains quintessentially Boston College. Neither the change nor the continuing identity would be possible without doing what the title of this presentation expresses, "imagining a heritage."

But now to turn to the second part of my remarks: what does all this history have to do with the Jesuit Institute whose inauguration we celebrate this weekend? I think it has much to do with it. Let me explain. To turn first to 1540 and the Society of Jesus itself, I hope that the Jesuit ethos or Jesuit spirituality might inform the Jesuit Institute with what Brian Daley, professor of theology at Weston School of Theology, calls three of the central characteristics of the fundamental Jesuit experience, the Spiritual Exercises. Those characteristics are wonder, freedom and practical commitment.[7] These three central elements of the Spiritual Exercises are: wonder at the goodness of God drawn from a contemplation of the world and history and God at work amidst them; freedom to be ourselves as God sees us, both dependent and, at the same time, self-determining; and a practical commitment to planning and action. I hope the Jesuit Institute is open to the wonder that asks questions not asked before. You already have an excellent first example of that in the project upon which the first Jesuit Institute research scholar, the Rev. Joseph A. Komonchak from Catholic University, will work next year. He is doing a major research project on "Theology and Modernity in Nineteenth and Twentieth Century Catholicism." Paul Claudel, some 70 years ago, saw eighteenth and nineteenth-century Catholicism not as an "intellectual crisis" but as "the tragedy of a starved imagination."[8] Father Komonchak says that the project will investigate "why it was that a religious tradition, which for most of its history had been open to contemporary cultures and [was characterized] by an effort to integrate faith and human knowledge, [now] seemed to regard the new culture of modernity with such profound suspicion and was content with a theology designed primarily for internal consumption . . . . The reasons for this, I will argue, lie less in definitions of theology or of science than in larger religious, cultural, political, and social assumptions." About that subject of theology and modernity the question has not previously been asked in that way. Secondly, I hope the Jesuit Institute will also live boldly the freedom to see ourselves as we really are, to engage in the serious inquiry and honest discussion and civil discourse that should characterize both a university and a research institute, to follow up without fear or favor the leads that wonder opens before its members. And thirdly, as to practical commitment, while the Institute is not meant to be an instrument of direct action, it is meant to do research that makes a difference and, to quote from the purposes and goals of the Institute, "to give serious scholarly attention to issues which are central to the goals of a university that is Catholic and Jesuit." What are those issues? What questions should you ask? You will have to decide that, but later I shall offer a few suggestions.

Because the Institute comes not only out of the history of the Jesuits but also the history of Jesuit education, let me turn now to what the Institute might draw from that long history of Jesuit educational institutions begun in 1547, and specifically from the reasons adduced by Ledesma for the Jesuit involvement in education and the experience of four centuries of such involvement. While the Institute is resolutely a research entity and not a teaching institution of itself, look for a moment at how well, for example, the research support for next year responds to the reasons given by Ledesma for Jesuit education.

When Ledesma says that the first purpose which the Society of Jesus had in engaging in the educational apostolate of schools was "because they supply us with many advantages for practical living," he finds an echo in the research proposal of Father Donald Kirby, S.J., which will look at how a project in teaching and assessing values might be applied to Jesuit and private higher education. When Ledesma says that such an education will "contribute to the right government of public affairs and the proper making of laws," the research project which Professor Richard Neilsen of the Carroll School of Management is doing on the possible convergence of Catholics and Quakers in their civil dialectic ethical reasoning surely responds to that purpose. When Ledesma speaks of such an education as giving "ornament, splendor and perfection to the rational nature of man," which might more contemporarily be put as the development of the total human person in the humanities and the sciences, Professor Judith Wilt's study of "God's Spies" in the novels of Virginia Woolf responds to that purpose. Finally, Ledesma's fourth purpose for Jesuit education as guiding people "most surely and easily to the achievement of their last end," or an education on a particular perspective on the ultimate nature and destiny of the human person beyond simply the human, can find its fulfillment at the core of the project of Professor Benjamin Braude, who asks of a Christian in the culture of the Muslim world the question: "How does a man of faith, an exclusive and universal faith, integrate and accept knowledge of a different faith?" In range and depth, all of these projects surely respond imaginatively both to Ledesma from the past and to the immediate present of the theme of the Jesuit Institute for 1989-1990, "Religious Faith and the

Searches for Knowledge." The theme is surely urgent and contemporary and it finds an echo this very next week and the week after as Raimon Panikkar gives the Gifford Lectures at Edinburgh on an analogous subject, "Trinity and Atheism: The Housing of the Divine in the Contemporary World."

To be sure, all of this work of the Jesuit Institute is taking place in the contemporary world, a world transformed by the Enlightenment, increasingly secular (not necessarily a bad word), and in many ways increasingly secularist too. For some people in our American culture, Christianity, the Society of Jesus, and a religiously committed university are as strange as Christianity in China at the time of Matteo Ricci. And the same is true vice-versa. If such a university and such a research institute wish to enter into dialogue with such a culture, as it is perfectly obvious they so wish to from the titles of the three panels for this present conference, "Family, Culture and Ethics," "Interrelating Religion and the Arts," and "Culture and Belief," then they may have to do as Ricci did by putting into effect Valignano's principles for entering into a relationship of inculturation.

You will recall those principles. First, we must have a sympathy and respect for the values of the people among whom we are working. One of the best gifts that the Jesuit Institute can give to Catholic culture and Jesuit presence in education in our times is to enable them increasingly to understand and respect our times, our institutions, our cultures today, and to be able to sympathize with the good in them, while being able also, when appropriate, to be distinctively countercultural out of our own distinctive heritages.

The second principle involved "a perfect command of the idiom or the language in which a culture is incarnated." How well do we know the cultural language of modern America? How well, indeed, do we know the languages in which contemporary Christians express their experiences of God, their reflections on that experience, their desires to understand their own religious experience, the Lord, the Church, Christ and his teachings? The Institute cannot simply repeat simply the old formulae. Instead, it must search for contemporary, ways of expressing the reality of revelation in the idiom of American culture, and for the best means of communicating it. If in the sixteenth century the printing press democratized learning, in the twentiety century, television has democratized experience. What are the implications for the languages of our culture?

The third and fourth of Valignano's principles were that science and scholarship, along with the world of serious writing and personal dialogue, were essential in exploring another culture and expressing one's own. Boston College has a reputation for taking the academic life seriously, for thinking that colleagueship and scholarship and research and good teaching are important, and that hard consistent study is necessary. They are among the greatest services that Boston College can itself render to the Church and to American culture in the present time and in the future. But how even more fortunate this place is in having such an entity as the Jesuit Institute which can devote itself directly to such scholarship and research, recognizing that, indeed, ideas have consequences. Look only at two examples, one 400 years old and the other contemporary. The ideas of Ricci and Valignano were, in effect, rejected, at least temporarily, by a Church too caught up in its Western ideas and Western structures, and that rejection by Rome brought on the near destruction of the Church in China. Only in the twentieth century Church were Ricci's insights fundamentally vindicated. As to the immediate past and our present times, we need only recall as an example how the scholarly research and publication of such places as the Dominican and Jesuit houses in France and Germany and Belgium over so many years did so much to shape the agenda and the results of Vatican II and the changes in the Church in the 25 years since that Council.

The fifth principle which Ricci sought to incarnate in his life, and which I hope will be part of the Jesuit Institute, was concern for and attention to those groups upon which society depends for its vision, leadership and cohesion. In the time of Valignano and Ricci in China, these were especially government officials and the scholarly communities. Other groups obviously would be included today in America, such as the professions or the labor unions or the media. But whatever they are, the Jesuit Institute should be in contact with and at the service of the larger community and of those particular communities and groups which make a difference in the Church and in American society. In such circumstances, how fortunate the Institute is to be related to a comprehensive university community and to be located in the Boston-Cambridge metropolitan area with the great panoply of other research and teaching institutions here. What kind of relationship will it have with those groups upon which society depends for its vision, leadership and cohesion?

Finally, the last of Valignano's principles dealt with the supreme importance of the example of the gospel lived out in one's life as the main witness to the credibility of the faith and of the Church. Every one of those earlier principles an enlightened, sympathetic, secular agency or non-believing person could and, perhaps, would adopt and put into practice. Of course, not everyone connected with the Jesuit Institute is going to be a Jesuit (fortunately for the Institute), nor, perhaps, will everyone connected with it share in the Catholic or Christian faith. But the Institute itself, in its attitudes and practices, will surely have to be witness in its own existence to the basic values of the gospel and to the possibility of incarnating those values in the details of the world in which we live and work. Always, in its own life and within its own membership, among the criteria for success of this Institute will be how its members treat one another and how they judge others, individuals and institutions, especially if those others seem to go contrary to its vision of itself. This is a task easier to describe than to do. To sum up, the Institute could do very little better than to take for itself and adapt to its particular circumstances those principles which Valignano and Ricci thought necessary if any serious work of inculturation in a civilization was to take place.

Let me turn now briefly to the relevance of that fourth and last date, 1789. It marked, as you will remember, the foundation of American Catholic higher education. That foundation was the product of the imagination of John Carroll, who had a vision of an educated American church. But even he could not have imagined how it has grown and prospered and developed far beyond even his dream. It has done so for a great variety of reasons, but among them are the facts of institutionalization and colleagueship. That is, the dream of a Church of educated Americans became a reality because the dream was actualized in a series of educational institutions, more than 200 of them all over the United States. In addition, they originally and especially drew upon the colleagueship of the members of the religious orders of men and women who conducted most of them. Increasingly, that colleagueship has widened and deepened to include lay women and men. This Jesuit Institute will have to ask itself how it organizes and institutionalizes itself and relates to United States' institutions, United States' life, the ethos of the United States, and how it establishes and fosters a real colleagueship among its members, Jesuit and lay and clerical.

Equally important, the Jesuit Institute will need the imagination (there we have that word again), to envision not short-term results from its research and writing activities but rather the kind of long-term results which have profound and lasting influences on American culture, perhaps even long after the lives of those who have done the research and writing. Think of the influences which de Tocqueville's book, *Democracy in America*, has had for 150 years.

To come now to the last part of my presentation: What kinds of research opportunities in American society today are there to which the Jesuit Institute might fittingly respond? The list could be infinite, but time for such research is finite and so is the time for this talk. So let me suggest, from a range of possibilities, the following examples, simply as examples which might especially respond to a serious imagining of the heritage of the Institute.

First, we confront today the continuing onrush of technology, and especially of information technology. How will American society respond to this? What are the implications for all of us in the developments described, for example, in the book recently written by Shoshana Zuboff, *The Age of the Smart Machine*? She argues that "advances in microelectronics, telecommunications, and computer science are producing a 'transformation of immense proportions,' comparable to the Industrial Revolution."[9] We know what the Industrial Revolution did to the whole world. Are we prepared to begin, at least to begin to imagine what the information technology revolution will do to our world, ourselves and our future generations? The Seminar on Jesuit Spirituality has already published a brief monograph on this subject by John Staudenmaier, S.J., "United States Technology and Adult Commitment,"[10] but the matter goes far, far beyond this first exploratory statement. It seems to me that the Jesuit Institute and, for instance, the Carroll School of Management might well together ask serious questions in this field.

Secondly, there is the whole question of ecumenism. It seemed so flourishing and so full of promise in the years immediately after Vatican II. Now it has, according to many observers, fallen into the doldrums. Is there a way in which we can look at it somewhat differently than before? Yves Congar, when thinking about the possibilities of variety within the unity of the Church, talked about "reconciled diversity," a formula which was produced in the Lutheran-Catholic dialogue. What might that formula do to resuscitate ecumenism? What theological and historical research is necessary here? How might the Boston College Institute of Religious Education and Pastoral Ministry and the Boston College Department of Theology work with the Jesuit Institute on this question?

A third area of possible research for the Jesuit Institute in the years to come might be how Jesuit education today is or ought to be involved in new and different ways with the humanities. Recently, Lynne Cheney, chairman of the National Endowment for the Humanities (NEH), spoke at a general session of the National Catholic Education Association convention and gave a report on "Strengthening the Nation's Memory: A Report on the Humanities in America." The Society of Jesus has been involved with the humanities in their literary manifestations throughout its history from the sixteenth through the eighteenth centuries. But it was rather suspicious of them in their plastic and representational forms in sculpture and painting in the old Society, and indifferent or hostile to them in the restored Society since the nineteenth century. What might the Jesuit Institute do to redress this imbalance: working, for example, with the College of Arts & Sciences? I say no more here lest I trespass on one or more of the panels of this inaugural conference, but there are surely many parts of this university which could enter into collaborative work.

Yet another example: With an increasingly aging population in the United States, might the Jesuit Institute find as a profitable area of inquiry the faith of older people? We have had much research and publication on the faith of children, the faith of adolescents, the faith of the young professional. But what about those people, increasingly large in number in American society, who come to the latter years of their life rich with experience and practiced in the living out of their religious convictions? What is their faith life? What has strengthened it? What has weakened it? What would they like to hand on to later generations? How might the Church and the Churches learn from this experience and this wisdom?

Another subject that needs serious scholarly investigation is the whole question of genetic engineering and its implications for Christian ethics, indeed for any kind of ethics, for moral theology, for the social structure of the American family, and for the health and welfare care of the American people. There are immense questions that invite, indeed almost demand, interdisciplinary research here.

Poverty and its repercussions on society and state and church, the still aching problem of widespread racism, the sexist treatment of women in society and in the Church are three more subjects asking for further work of the kind which the Institute proposes to do. If one would seek to do research on explicitly Jesuit topics, let me suggest that the whole history of the work of the Society in Eastern Europe from the sixteenth century on is a barely touched area. The understanding of the Jesuit Constitutions through the centuries is another topic; a first international meeting on that is to be held in France in October, 1989. And then, extraordinary as it may seem, for the greatest and most important general next to Ignatius in the history of the Society, Claudio Acquaviva, there exists no serious biography in any language.

As a last example of a particular subject of investigation: What does tradition really mean and what influence does it have in American civil society, in American culture, in American religious theory, institutions and practice, in the Catholic Church in America? What will tradition mean in the future in an increasingly technologically-oriented society? What might tradition mean if we looked at it not so much as an act of handing on the past but as an act which is essentially future-oriented and which, therefore, demands imagination? What will tradition mean if we look at it in the light of Karl Rahner's statement that the Second Vatican Council is at root, in a way that is just gropingly seeking to find itself, the first official self-realization of the Church as a world church? Imagine what might happen if we took seriously the fact that, after all, "the Church is . . . essentially a mystery, in whose proclamation and service the institution finds its sole justification."[11]

At the final event of celebration of Boston College's one hundred and twenty-fifth anniversary, the Mass of thanksgiving last November, the provincial of the New England Province of the Society of Jesus, Father Robert Manning, spoke forcefully on the theme of collaboration between the Jesuit community and all of the groups represented by those who participated in that Mass. As an overarching theme, the Jesuit Institute might well choose to look at that question of collaboration, collaboration as the context of work together, collaboration as the prerequisite for community, collaboration as the underlying content of the work of the Institute. And, in practice, it might quite deliberately, right from the beginning, seek to do collaborative work with other of the Jesuit colleges and universities and with several other Jesuit research centers around the United States.

I may have left you with enough subjects to begin the work of the Jesuit Institute. I hope so. Much more do I hope that you, the members of the Institute and its friends and supporters, will have far more and far better suggestions that I for the work that it might do in the years to come.

As I began these remarks, so let me end them. The founding of the Jesuit Institute is an extraordinary event. It involves, as I said, the imagining of a heritage, the institutionalizing of the consequences of that imagination and the colleagueship necessary to bring that imagination to reality. That heritage is rich and complex. It includes the ethos of the Society of Jesus, the establishment of education as a Jesuit work, the attempt to address what some call a post-Christian civilization but what is at least a civilization increasingly as unfamiliar with the traditional terms and categories of Christianity as Ricci's China was totally unfamiliar with them, and as a last part of that heritage, it involves the whole American context of the Jesuit endeavor in higher education, now 200 years old. All of this is part of the heritage upon which the Jesuit Institute can draw for its future. We cannot predict that future but we can look to it with the last words of Matteo Ricci, after a life spent in so unusual and splendid an endeavor as his, stirring our minds, our hearts, our imagination: "It will not be without great effort and many perils, but I leave you standing before a door open to great accomplishments."

Notes

1. Thomas Fuller in Robert E. McNally, S.J., *The Unreformed Church* (New York: Sheed & Ward, 1968) 19.

2. See Jules Toner, S.J., "The Deliberation That Started the Jesuits," *Studies in the Spirituality of Jesuits*, 6/4 (June, 1974); for the official document of papal approval, see *"Regimini Militantis Ecclesiae"* of Pope Paul III, Sept. 27, 1540 in *Institutum Societatis Jesu*, vol. 1 (Florence, 1893).

3. A useful edition of the Spiritual Exercises is in David L. Fleming, S.J., *The Spiritual Exercises of St. Ignatius: A Literal Translation and a Contemporary Reading*. (St. Louis: Institute of Jesuit Sources, 1989).

4. Diego Ledesma, S.J., *De Ratione et Ordine Studiorum Collegii Romani* in *Monumenta Paedogogica Societatis Jesu Quae Primam Rationem Studiorum anno 1586 editam praecessere*. (Madrid, 1901) 345.

5. Pedro de Ribadeneyra, S.J., *Tratado en el cual se da razon del instituto de la religion de la Compania de Jesus* (Madrid: Colegio de la Compania, 1605 quoted by Brian Daley, S.J. in *Splendor and Wonder*, edited by William J. O'Brien (Washington: Georgetown University Press, 1989) 3.

6. For Ricci, see Jonothan Spence, *The Memory Palace of Matteo Ricci* (New Haven: Viking Press, 1984) and the older but still interesting general account, Vincent Cronin, *The Man From the West* (New York: Dutton 1955). For Valignano, see Josef Franz Schutte, S.J., *Valignano's Mission Principles for Japan*, translated by John J. Coyne, S.J., 2 vols. (St. Louis: The Institute of Jesuit Sources, 1980 and 1985).

7. Brian E. Daley, S.J., "'Splendor and Wonder': Ignatian Mysticism and the Ideals of Liberal Education" in *Splendor and Wonder*, 7-9.

8. Paul Claudel in Eugene Kennedy, *Tomorrow's Catholics, Yesterday's Church* (New York: Harper and Row, 1988) xi.

9. *Harvard Magazine* (November-December, 1988) 56.

10. See John Staudenmaier, S.J., "United States Technology and Adult Commitment," *Studies in the Spirituality of Jesuits*, 19/1 (January, 1987).

11. Kennedy, *op cit.* 8.

The Family, Democratic Politics and the Question of Authority

Jean Bethke Elshtain
Centennial Professor of Political Science
Vanderbilt University

The architecture of this essay is as follows: I begin by assaying our contemporary "crisis of authority" as it has been tagged by a number of commentators representing diverse philosophic and political communities. Second, I offer a brief narrative of democratic authority, the family, and politics as an inherited dilemma that continues to haunt current reflections. Third, I state a strong case for familial authority and its relation to democratic politics that ushers into a more ambiguous endorsement of this authority in light of challenges to the norms and practices that constitute the family.*

A caveat to forestall one predictable criticism: I recognize that there is no such thing as *the* family as a constant, unchanging object that corresponds to a universal form. Families are sets of social relations that vary with time and place. But in and of itself this doesn't tell us very much that is interesting. What is interesting, for the civic philosopher, is the family as a site of moral and political discourse; the family as a complex representation that signifies by its presence or its absence within alternative traditions of inquiry; the family as a remarkably stubborn yet adaptive repository of human hopes, dreams, and conflicts; the family as concrete human ties and loyalties which modern society either sustains or suborns.

---

*This is the third and probably not final version of the argument elaborated in the pages to follow. One earlier variant appeared in G. Scarre, ed. Children and Politics (Cambridge University Press, 1989.) My emphases and language here are markedly different from its precursor.

21

The crisis of authority assayed

The political and social theorists and activists who assume a crisis of authority in democracy or the family, or would precipitate a crisis to promote change, frame their discourse through such questions as: Is "democratic authority" an oxymoron? If democratic authority is a possibility, is the family compatible with it? If not, should the family be made to conform to the standards of democratic political authority? Or should we, instead, restore older notions of authority for families and politics that modernity has destroyed or eroded? Have we got too much authority or not enough? Are we in decline or do great possibilities lie ahead if we have the political will to change what must be changed? And so on.

I will explore the contours of contemporary crisis discourse as background to my defense of familial authority, by taking up, briefly, exemplars of the restorationist and reformist positions as articulated by Robert Nisbet and Jürgen Habermas, respectively.

Robert Nisbet, in a number of important works, most notably, *The Twilight of Authority*, argues that the loss of authority in the contemporary age culminates in the atomization of society, the breakdown of community, the rise of unreason, and opposition to the values of due process, privacy, and rights.[1] This potpourri of social ills is, for Nisbet, inseparable from the rise of liberalism and the victory of an instrumentalist and relativistic social ethos. At base, this crisis is moral, resulting when human life, public and private, is ruthlessly desacralized. According to Nisbet, this crisis of authority began *first* in the political sphere and then spread to "other areas of institutional life." He writes:

> By a strange law of social behavior, decline actually causes attack. Let a government, economic enterprise, or church reach a certain point of enervation, . . . and it is virtually certain that some kind of assault will be mounted on it . . . . It is in these terms, I believe, that we are obligated to see contemporary assaults upon the historic family and upon the ties

and roles which the family has sustained for so many thousands of years.[2]

A prior weakening of the family's authority *causes* revolts against it rather than the reverse. Put under pressure from superior external forces, political and economic, the family has nearly succumbed. Precisely for this reason, it becomes a target for rebels who can combat the supra-structures who are the real culprits. Misguidedly, social rebels wind up deepening the crisis they hope to resolve.

Jürgen Habermas would find much of Nisbet's argument a long lament over the inability of conservatives to hold back the tides of social change. Habermas does, however, share Nisbet's sense of crisis which, in Habermasian language, gets construed as a breakdown of "system integration" so great it poses a threat to "social integration." System integration or, we might say, stability is menaced by a driven process of production and accumulation that creates intolerable contradictions within the political and socio-cultural system. In other words, old norms give way and alienation and anomie result.[3] When this confluence of forces culminates in a "motivation crisis" that undermines allegiance to the standards of democratic order and its constitutive principles, one confronts, as does the modern West, a full-blown crisis of legitimation.

The political projects that flow from each author's crisis mirror one another: Nisbet urges us to restore a resacralized exercise of traditional authority in familial, political and economic spheres— we must rediscover belief; Habermas wants to create a social order that more fully deserves, hence receives, the critical allegiance of its members—we should carry even further rationalism's challenge to belief. Nisbet endorses mystery and murkiness in our arrangements so that they are less susceptible to arrogant tinkering; Habermas extols an "ideal speech situation" of perfectly symmetrical, transparent discourse as a precondition for a new, authoritative consensus.

Crisis discourse presents us with a picture of wrongs to be righted. The political analyst who shares the language and rhetoric of crisis is likely to overdraw our dilemmas the better to mobilize our will in one direction or another. The attractions of this approach are many, including the promise that social ills can be cured once the sites of "infection" are located and treated. Each wants to solve *the* problem. But that problem is one they ironically shore up, given their tacit commitment to the very old idea that there can be only one authority principle operative within a political and social order if it is to be well governed. Nisbet and Habermas would bring the world into line with the contours of an argument about what it ought to be or must be unless we want continuing conflicts and crises. The roots of their concern lie in the history of the uneasy relationship between democratic authority and the family.

Democratic Authority and the Family: The Construction of a Dilemma

The suspicions democrats have and have had about traditional authority, lodged in kings and chiefs, in popes and lords, is easily understood. For democracy requires self-governing and self-regulating citizens rather than obedient subjects. Being in a position of authority in democracy is the temporary holding of an office at the sufferance of those who delegate powers to the office-holder.

The background features of democratic authority and its exercise emerged unevenly over several centuries as late medieval and early modern cosmologies faltered.[4] The features I have in mind include the principle that citizens possess inalienable rights. Possession of such rights empowers citizens to offer authoritative assent to the laws, rules, and practices that constitute democratic politics, including those procedural guarantees that afford them protection against abuses of the authority they have themselves authorized.

Equality between and among citizens was assumed from the beginning on the part of liberals and democrats; indeed, the citizen was, by definition, equal to any other *qua* citizen. (Not everyone, of course, could be a citizen: another ongoing dilemma.) Liberal and democratic citizenship required the creation of persons with the qualities of mind and spirit necessary for civic participation. This creation of citizens was seen as neither simple nor automatic by early liberal theorists, leading many to insist upon a structure of education tied to a particular understanding of "the sentiments." This education should usher into a moral autonomy that stresses self-chosen obligations, thereby casting further suspicion upon all relations, practices, and loyalties deemed unchosen, involuntary, or natural.

Within such accounts of civic authority, the family emerged as a problem. For one does not enter a family through free consent; one is born into the world unwilled and unchosen by oneself, beginning life as a helpless and dependent infant. Eventually one reaches "the age of consent." But in the meantime one is a child, not a citizen. This vexed liberal and democratic theorists, some of whom believed, at least abstractly, that the completion of the democratic ideal required bringing all of social life under the sway of a single democratic authority principle.

The historic period most critical as backdrop for our current conflict over authority, democracy and the family is rooted in the sixteenth and seventeenth-century shift from patriarchal to liberal-contractarian discourse. Patriarchalist discourse in its paradigmatic form (I have in mind Robert Filmer's *Patriarcha*) was preeminently about authority, construing a tight case for authority as single, absolute, patriarchal, natural and political. In Filmer's world there is no drawing of distinctions between public and private, family and politics; indeed, there is no private sphere (in the sense of a realm demarcated from political life), nor political sphere (in the sense of a realm diverging from the exigencies of the private world) at all. Power, authority and obedience are fused within the original grant of dominion by God to Adam at creation. Within Filmer's unitary theory of authority there are only subjects, save, perhaps, for the divine right monarch alone. Each father lords it over his wife, his children and his servants in his own little kingdom. But he, in turn, is subjected to the First Father, the lordly king.

Countering the strong traditional case for God-given patriarchal authority proved relatively easy for liberals and democrats where their visions of civil society were concerned, but was trickier by far where their transformed notions of authority seemed to challenge the family. Was a familial form dominated by patriarchal presumptions, however softened in practice, suitable or legitimate within a civic world framed by presumptions of consent? If liberals sought to end a condition of perpetual political childhood, were they required to eliminate childhood itself? A strong version of the liberal ideal, "free consent" from birth, was deeply problematic given the nature of human infants.[5] Liberal contractarians were often cautious in carrying their political principles into domestic life, some contenting themselves with contractarianism in politics and economics, traditionalism in families, not however, without considerable discursive maneuvering.[6] Filmer's caustic query to his liberal interlocutors concerning whether people sprang up like "so many mushrooms" and his incredulous insistency: "How can a child express consent?" continued to haunt liberals, in part because they shared with Filmer the presumption that authority must be single in form if a society is to be coherent and orderly.

John Locke, more subtle than many early liberal thinkers, softened demands for relentless consistency in social practices and norms, arguing instead for the coexistence of diverse authoritative social forms and practices. Conjugal society must come into being through consent on the part of two adults. But "parental" or "paternal" power within the family (Locke recognizes both, but privileges the latter), could not serve as a model for the liberal polity any more than the norms constituting civil society could provide an apposite model for families. Locke strips the father-husband of patriarchal absolutism by denying him sovereignty, which includes the power of life and death. That prerogative is reserved *only* to democratically legitimated public authority. A father's power is "conjugal . . . not Political" and these two are "perfectly distinct and separate . . . built upon so different Foundations and given to so different Ends . . . ."[7] The child's status is that of not-yet-adult, hence not part of the consensual civil order. But the education of the child into moral sentiments is vital to that wider order. Locke avoids the seductions of the patriarchal authority principle as an all-encompassing norm by refusing to launch a mimetic project that mirrors patriarchalism. That is, he does not substitute an overarching liberal authority principle that turns the family into an explicit political society governed by the same principles that prevailed in liberal public life.

The lack of perfect congruence between political and familial modes of authority continued to vex post-Lockean liberal and democratic thinkers. Whether because the position of women who, having reached the age of consent, could enter freely into a marriage relation only to find future consent foreclosed, or because the family itself was a blemish to those who foresaw the ultimate triumph of rationalism and contract in all spheres of human existence, liberals returned over and over to relations between the family and politics.

This culminates in the nineteenth century when John Stuart Mill, in contrast to Locke, insists that familial and civic orders be drawn into a tight mesh with one another. For Mill, the family remained a despotic sphere governed by a "law of force" whose "odious source" was rooted in pre-enlightened and barbaric epochs. By revealing the origins of family relations, thus bringing out their "true" character, Mill hoped to demonstrate that the continued subjection of women blunts social progress. He proposed a leap into relations of "perfect equality" between the sexes as the only way to complete the teleology of liberal individualism and equality, to assure the promise of Progress.

In his tract, *The Subjection of Women*, Mill argued that his contemporaries, male and female alike, were tainted by the atavisms of family life with its illegitimate, because unchosen and pre-rational, male authority, and its illegitimate, because manipulative and irrational, female quests for private power.[8] The family will become a school in the virtues of freedom only when parents live together without power on one side or obedience on the other. Power, for Mill, is repugnant: true liberty must reign in all spheres. But what about the children? Mill's children emerge as rather abstract concerns: blank slates on which parents must encode the lessons of obedience towards the end of inculcating authoritatively the lessons of freedom. Stripped of undemocratic authority and privilege, the parental union serves as a model of democratic probity.[9]

Mill's paeon to liberal individualism is interestingly contrasted to Alexis de Tocqueville's concrete observations of family life in nineteenth-century America, a society already showing the effects of the extension of democratic, and the breakdown of patriarchal and Puritan, norms and practices. The political fathers of Tocqueville's America were fathers in a different mode, at once stern but forgiving, strong but flexible. They listened to their children and humored them. They educated as well as demanded obedience. Like the new democratic father, the American political leader did not lord it over his people. Citizens were not required to bend the knee or stand transfixed in awe. The leader was owed respect and, if he urged a course of action upon his fellow citizens following proper consultation and procedural requirements, they had a patriotic duty to follow.

Tocqueville's discerning eye perceived changing public and private relationships in liberal, democratic America. Although great care was taken "to trace two clearly distinct lines of action for the two sexes," women, in their domestic sphere, nowhere occupied a loftier position of honor and importance, Tocqueville claimed.[10] The mother's familial role was enhanced, given her essential civic vocation as the chief inculcator of democratic values in her offspring. "No free communities ever existed without morals and, as I observed . . . , morals are the work of 'women.' "[11]

Although the father was the family's "natural head," his authority was neither absolute nor arbitrary. In contrast to the patriarchal authoritarian family where the parent not only had a "natural right" but acquired a "political right" to command his children, in a democratic family the right and authority of parents is a *natural right* alone.[12] This natural authority presents no problem for democratic practices as Tocqueville construes democracy, in contrast to Mill. Indeed, the fact that the "right to command" is natural, not political, signifies its special and temporary nature: once the child is self-governing, the right dissolves. In this way natural, legitimate paternal authority and maternal moral education reinforce a political order that values flexibility, freedom, and the absence of absolute rule but requires, as well, order and stability.

Popular columnists and "child experts" in Tocqueville's America emphasized kindness and love as the preferred technique of child nurture. Obedience was still seen as necessary—to parents, elders, God, "just government and one's conscience." But the child was no longer construed as a depraved, sin-ridden, stiff-necked creature who needed harsh, unyielding instruction and reproof. A more benign view of the child's nature emerged as notions of infant depravity faded together with Puritan patriarchalism. The problem of discipline grew more, rather than less, complex. Parents were enjoined to get obedience without corporal punishment and rigid methods, using reason and affection, issuing their commands in gentle but firm voices, insisting quietly on their authority lest contempt and chaos reign in the domestic sphere.

Tocqueville's image of the "democratic family" sees children both as ends in themselves and as means to the end of a well-ordered family and polity. A widespread moral consensus reigned in the America of that era, a kind of Protestant civic religion. When this consensus began to corrode under the force of rapid social change (and there are analogues to the American story in all modern democracies), certainties surrounding familial authority as a secure locus for the creation of democratic citizens were shaken as well.

If no form of social authority can any longer be taken for granted in light of continuing challenges to the norms that govern both familial and civil sphere, a case *for* family authority as a good in itself and as one background feature that makes possible democratic society becomes more difficult to mount unless one opts for restorationism, or celebrates high rationalist hopes that the time is finally ripe to bring the entire social order under the sway of wholly voluntarist norms. If restorationists long to return traditional norms to their once unambiguous status, the voluntarist option is problematic given its implied intent to nullify the moral and social significance of all "unchosen" purposes and obligations. If one finds both these alternatives unrealistic or undesirable, the task of articulating a defense of familial authority within, and for, a social world whose members no longer share one overriding conception of the good life, nor repose deep faith in the future of human institutions, becomes ever more exigent.

I move in two directions in the section below. First, I launch a strong case in behalf of family authority. Second, I put questions to this strong case by taking note of objections to it that yield, in turn, a more ambiguous set of reflections and affirmations. Complicating my argument in this way offers an opportunity to evaluate whether or not the strong case remains compelling, or, alternatively, whether a softened defense of familial authority better serves the social goods at stake in the long run.[13]

Democratic Authority and the Family: The Strong Case

Familial authority, though apparently at odds with the governing presumptions of democratic authority, is nonetheless part of the constitutive background required for the survival and flourishing of democracy. Family relations could not exist without family authority and these relations remain the best way we know anything about how to create human beings with a developed capacity to give ethical allegiance to the background presumptions and principles of democratic society. Family authority structures the relationship between adult providers, nurturers, educators, and disciplinarians and dependent children who slowly acquire capacities for independence. Modern parental authority is shared by mother and father. (Some readers may take strong exception to this claim, arguing that the family is patriarchal, even today; or that the authority of the mother is *less* decisive than that of the father; or that

Mill was right. Children, however, exhibit little doubt that their mothers are powerful and authoritative, though perhaps not in ways identical to fathers.) This ideal of parental equality in relation to children does *not* presuppose an identity between mother and father. Each can be more or less a private or a public person, yet be equal in relation to children in the way here described.

What makes family authority distinctive is the sense of stewardship internal to it, the recognition that parents undertake continuing solemn obligations and responsibilities. The authority of the parent is special, limited, and particular. Parental authority, like any form of authority, may be abused but unless it exists the activity of parenting itself is impossible. The authority of parents in relation to children is implicated in that moral education required for democratic citizenship, the creation of a democratic political morality. The *Herzenbildung*—education of the heart—which takes place in families should not, however, be seen as but one item in a larger political agenda. To construe it as such is to treat the family merely instrumentally, affirming it only insofar as it can be shown to serve some externally defined set of purposes. That the family underscores the authoritative rules and norms that govern the wider order may be true. But it also offers alternatives to the actual policies and programs a public order may throw up at any given point in time.

The intense loyalties, obligations, and moral imperatives nurtured in families may clash with the requirements of public authority, for example, when young men refuse to serve in an unjust war because this runs counter to the religious beliefs instilled in their families. This, too, is vital for democracy. Democracy emerged as a form of revolt. Keeping alive a potential locus for revolt, for particularity, for difference, sustains democracy in the long run. It is no coincidence that all twentieth-century totalitarian orders labored to destroy the family as a locus of identity and meaning apart from the state. Totalitarian politics strives to consume all of life, to allow for a single *public* identity, to destroy private life, to require that individuals identify only with the state rather than with specific others—family, friends, comrades.

Family authority within a democratic, pluralistic order, does not exist in a direct, homologous relation to the principles of civil society. To establish an identity between public and private lives and purposes would weaken, not strengthen, democratic life over-all. For children need particular, intense relations with specific adult others to learn to make distinctions and choices as adults. The child, if confronted prematurely with the "right to choose," should parents abnegate their authority, or should the child be situated too soon inside anonymous, institutional contexts that minimize points of special, unique contact and trust with specific adult others, is likely to be less capable of choosing later on. To become a being capable of posing alternatives, one requires a sure and certain place from which to start. In Mary Midgley's words: "Children . . . have to live *now* in a particular culture; they must take some attitude to the nearest things right away."[14] The social form best suited to provide children with a trusting, determinate sense of place and ul-timately a "self" is the family. Indeed, it is only through identifica-tion with concrete others that the child can later identify with non-familial human beings and come to see herself as a member of a wider human community.

Family authority is inseparable from parental care, protection, and concern. In the absence of such ties, familial feelings would not be displaced throughout a wider social network—they would, in-stead, be vitiated, perhaps lost altogether. And without the human ties and bonds that the activity of parenting makes possible, a more general sense of "brotherhood" and "sisterhood" cannot emerge.

The nature and scope of parental authority alters over time. Children learn that being a child is not a permanent condition. One of the lessons the family teaches is that no authority on this earth is omnipotent, unchanging, and absolute. Working through familial authority, as the child struggles for identity, requires that she ques-tion authority more generally. Examples of authoritarian parents do not disconfirm this ideal case; they do, however, point to the fact that family authority, like any constitutive principle, is subject to deformation and abuse in particular cases. Granting the possibility for abuse, sustaining familial authority (meaning that of both parents in their relations to children, as well as families in their relation to the wider social order) keeps alive that combination of obligation and duty, freedom and dissent characteristic of democratic life.

The stance of the democrat towards family authority resists easy characterization. It involves a rejection of any ideal of political and familial life that absorbs all social relations under a single authority principle. Families are not democratic polities. With its concreteness, its insistence on the unique and the non-instrumental, the family helps us to hold intact the respective goods and ends of exclusive relations and arrangements. Any further erosion of that ethical life embodied in the family bodes ill for democracy. For example, we can experience the plight of *homelessness* as a human tragedy *only* because we cherish an ideal of what it means to make and to have a home. Thus, a defense of the family, rather than ushering in rigid traditionalism, can help to sustain a commitment to "do something" about a whole range of social problems.

Abusive families are a particular tragedy. The loss of the family and its characteristic forms of authority and relations would be a general debacle from which we would not soon recover. The replacements for parents and families would not be a happy, consensual world of children co-equal with adults but one in which children became clients of institutionally powerful social bureaucrats and engineers of all sorts for whom they would serve as so much grist for the mill of extra-familial schemes and ambitions.

The ideal democratic family here sketched is a feature of a democratic *Sittlichkeit*, one vital and necessary arena of concrete social life and ethical existence. But it may serve as well as a "launching pad" into more universal commitments, a civic *Moralität*. The child who emerges from such a family is more likely to be capable of acting in the world as a complex moral being, one part of, yet somewhat detached from, the immediacy of his or her own concerns and desires, given the complex negotiations he or she has internalized as part of growing up.

Democratic Authority and the Family: Ambiguous Recognitions

The strong case presumes a family that is secure, or can be made secure, in its authoritative role, a family that serves as the bearer of a clear telos. This is spine-stiffening stuff. But it presupposes a wider social surround that no longer exists in its paradigmatic form. American society ceased long ago to endorse unambiguously the shouldering of family obligations and to locate honor in long-term moral responsibilities. The authoritative norms that sustain the strong case have fallen under relentless pressures that promote individualistic, mobile, and tentative relations between self and others. Modern subjects are enjoined to remain as untrammeled as possible in order to attain individual goals and to enjoy their "freedom." Constraints grow more onerous than they were when it was anticipated that everyone would share them—all women, almost without exception, would become mothers; all men, almost without exception, would become supportive fathers. Located inside a wider ethos that no longer affords clear-cut moral and social support for familial relations and responsibilities, young people, unsurprisingly, choose in growing numbers to postpone or evade these responsibilities.

In acknowledging these transformations, the case for familial authority is softened but not abandoned. Taking account of shifts in the social ethos does not mean that one succumbs to them as if they comprised a new authoritative norm simply by virtue of their existence. But some alterations are warranted, including articulation of less dauntingly rigorous normative requirements for being a "parent" than those implied by the strong argument. The changes I have in mind here are *not* facile reassurances that modern human beings can be unfettered individualists and encumbered parents in some happy, perfect, harmonious configuration. For parental authority both *constrains* and *makes possible*, locating mothers and fathers in the world in a way that *must* be different from that of non-parenting adults. This need not lock parents into a dour notion of their duty that encourages them to overstate their power to shape their children, and their responsibility for doing so. The modern family is a porous institution, one open to a variety of external images and influences. Parents are no longer the sole moral guardians and one's defense of familial authority must take this into account, assessing its meaning in the structure of domestic life.

Critics of family authority might continue the challenge by insisting that even this softened case is "arbitrary" in several ways: because it privileges procreative heterosexual unions, thereby excluding a variety of other intimate arrangements, whether "non-exclusive," "open" marriages and families, or homosexual unions, from its purview; because it maintains a notion of the child as a dependent who requires discipline and restriction, thus shoring up paternalism ostensibly in behalf of children but really to deny them their rights; because it limits parental social choices by stressing dependability, trust, and loyalty to the exclusion of adventure, unpredictability, and openness; because it constructs a case for ethical development that is self-confirming in assuming that a set of authoritative norms is essential to personal life.

Perhaps, this critic might go on, behavior modification is a less strenuous and more effective shaper of a child's actions. Perhaps children thrown early on out of the home and into a group context emerge less burdened by individual conscience and moral autonomy, and hence are freer to act creatively without incessant, guilt-ridden ruminations about responsibility and consequence than those children reared in the family idealized in the strong case. Perhaps children who learn, at an early age, to be cynical and *not* to trust adults will be better skeptics, better prepared to accept the rapid changes of modernity, than the trusting, emotionally-bonded, slowly-maturing children in the family sketched.

I will concede that a reflective brief in behalf of family authority should recognize explicitly that every set of authoritative norms will contain some contingent features, contingent "in the sense that, while they are indispensable to this way of life, there are other forms of living . . . in which this special set would not be necessary."[15] But "conventional" or "contingent" need not mean "arbitrary." In the absence of any authoritative rules and relations, the social world would be more rather than less dominated by violence, coercion, or crass manipulation.

Take, for example, the incest taboo. The incest taboo can be construed as wholly arbitrary, as a number of radical social critics have claimed, translating that to mean both "illegitimate" and "indefensible," contrary to individual freedom of expression and action. Exposing its arbitrariness, they would liberate children from paternalistic despotism and parents from an ancient superstition. Chafing at restrictions of sexual exploration that construct strong normalizing limits and that establish sharp boundaries between familial and extra-familial sexuality, as well as between adults and children inside families, these anti-authoritarians celebrate total freedom of sexual exploration as an alternative.

The mistake on the part of the anti-incest taboo protagonists is not their insistence that we recognize the conventional features of our social arrangements, but their conviction that such exposure requires elimination of the rules or practices in question. In assuming that a viable mode of social existence might come into being and flourish in the absence of authoritative restrictions, the "antis" emerge as naive and dangerous. They would open up social life to more rather than less brutalization, including targeting children (in the example under purview) as acceptable resources for adult sexual manipulation and coercion. Continued authoritative acceptance of the incest taboo implicates one in a powerful, normative standard, it is true. But that standard is necessary to sustain a social good—protecting children from systematic abuse by the more powerful. Parental power is limited and constrained. That is why we condemn and punish abusive parents. Adult power, shorn of the internal moral limits of the incest taboo, would become more generalized, less accountable, and dangerously unlimited.

A second radical criticism holds, as I have suggested, that in defending the family and intergenerational ties, one privileges a restrictive ideal of sexual and intimate relations. There are within contemporary American life those who believe that a society can and should stay equally open to all, or alternative, arrangements, treating "lifestyles" as so many identical peas in a pod. To be sure, families in modernity coexist with those who live another way, whether heterosexual and homosexual unions that are by choice or by definition childless, communalists who diminish individual parental authority in favor of the preeminence of the group, and so on.

But the recognition and acceptance of plural possibilities does not mean each alternative is equal to every other with reference to specific social goods. No social order has ever existed that did not endorse certain activities and practices as preferable to others. Every social order forges terms of inclusion and exclusion. Ethically responsible challenges to our terms of exclusion and inclusion push towards a loosening but not a wholesale negation in our normative endorsement of intergenerational family life. In defining family authority, then, one acknowledges that one is *privileging* relations of a particular kind when and where certain social goods are at stake.

Those excluded by, or who exclude themselves from, this authoritative norm should not be denied social space and tolerance for their own practices. And it is possible that if what were at stake were, say, seeking out and identifying those creations of self that enhance an aesthetic construction of life and sensibility, the romantic bohemian or rebel would get higher marks than the Smith Family of Freemont, Nebraska. Nevertheless, we should be cautious about going too far in the direction of a wholly-untrammeled pluralism with reference to authoritative evaluations, lest we become so vapid that we are no longer capable of distinguishing between the moral weightiness of, say, polishing one's Porsche and sitting up all night with an ill child. The intergenerational family remains central and critical in nurturing recognitions of human frailty, morality and finitude, in inculcating moral limits and constraints. A revamped defense of family authority, then, takes account of challenges to its normalizing features and opens it to ambiguities and paradox.

As I conclude, it seems that the worries of historic liberal thinkers about family's anomalous position within a civic world governed by contractarian and voluntarist norms were misplaced. Ironically, what such analysts *feared* is what I here *endorse*: a form of family authority that does *not* mesh perfectly with democratic authority principles, yet remains vital to the sustaining of a diverse and morally decent culture. This is an example of one of many paradoxes that social life throws up, and that civic philosophers would be well advised to recognize and to nourish. The discordancies embodied in the uneasy co-existence of family and democratic authority sustain those struggles over identity, purpose, and meaning that are the very stuff of democratic life.

To resolve the untidiness of our public and private relations by either reaffirming unambiguously a set of unitary, authoritative norms or eliminating all such norms as arbitrary is to jeopardize the social goods that democratic and familial authority, paradoxical in relation to one another, promise—to men and women as parents and citizens and to their children.

Notes

1. Robert Nisbet, *The Twilight of Authority* (Oxford: Oxford University Press, 1975).

2. *Ibid.*, 80.

3. Jürgen Habermas, *The Legitimation Crisis* (Boston: Beacon Press, 1973).

4. This is not to say that all features of these ontologies are, in principle, no longer available to us. Many continue to structure their

lives primarily in and through such ontologies of faith, but not, I would argue, without conflict.

5. Hobbes is here, as elsewhere, an anomalous thinker, fusing absolutism with consent in all spheres, including the family, and accepting coerced "choice" as legitimate.

6. On this subject, see Mary Lyndon Shanley, "Marriage Contract and Social Contract in Seventeenth-Century English Political Thought," in Jean Bethke Elshtain, editor, *The Family in Political Thought* (Amherst, Massachusetts: University of Massachusetts Press, 1982) 80-95.

7. John Locke, *Two Treatises of Government,* edited by Peter Laslett (New York: New American Library, 1965) 357.

8. John Stuart Mill, *The Subjection of Women* (Greenwich, CT: Fawcett, 1970).

9. Not even Mill took the argument for consent to its *reductio ad absurdum* in some recent versions of "children's liberation." See Richard W. Krouse, "Patriarchal Liberalism and Beyond: From John Stuart Mill to Harriet Taylor," in Elshtain, ed., *The Family in Political Thought* (145-172).

10. Alexis de Tocqueville, *Democracy in America,* ed. Phillips Bradley, 2: 223.

11. *Ibid.,* 2:209. There is an echo of Rousseau in this.

12. *Ibid.,* 2: 203-204.

13. William E. Connolly, in "Modern Authority and Ambiguity," *Politics and Ambiguity* (Madison, Wisconsin: University of Wisconsin Press, 1987) 127-142, argues that ambiguity is necessary to any defense of authority in modernity.

14. Mary Midgley, *Beast and Man. The Roots of Human Nature,* (Ithaca, NY: Cornell University Press, 1978) 291.

15. Connolly, "Modern Authority and Ambiguity," 138.

Family, Culture, and Ethics: Their Interaction and Impact upon African Americans and White Americans

Preston N. Williams
Houghton Professor of
Theology and Contemporary Change
The Harvard Divinity School

Family, culture, and ethics, the three terms to be discussed in this paper, are very general designations for the manner in which human beings relate to each other, devise systems and patterns to give meaning to their lives together, and order that life in normative ways. Together, the realities the terms name make up much but not all of a person's life and their proper development ensures for the possessor a good and righteous life. It is not surprising, consequently, that individuals (including ourselves) seek to know fully these relationships, meanings, and rules, for upon that knowledge rests our opportunity to obtain fulfillment in living. Yet it should be clear to earnest seekers like ourselves, as well as others, that it is exceedingly difficult to know all that is entailed in grasping and understanding these important aspects of human life. Because this is so, in this paper I must limit my discussion of these concepts. I have chosen therefore to examine the relationship that exists among them and the manner in which it should be ordered in order to achieve wholeness in life and to provide guidance to those who seek to create a just and good society. I have chosen this focus because it has been an object of public policy concern in respect to the American family, especially the African American portion of that family.

The introduction of a concern with the American family points to another necessary aspect of any consideration of the concepts of family, culture, and ethic, namely that any adequate attempt to understand them involves inevitably a discussion of society. The Roman Catholic Church has long maintained that the family is the basic unit in society. My interpretation of that assertion differs somewhat from that of the Roman Catholic Church, but the fact that the church teaches that doctrine suggests that the family needs to be viewed in the context of a society. It also alerts us to the wisdom and necessity of considering culture and ethic in their societal context. The relating of family to society is often made in order to enhance the significance of family and to indicate its priority over or parity with the state and other social institutions. The argument contends that whole and healthy families are absolutely essential for whole and healthy cultures, ethics, and societies. The family must be whole and healthy in order to achieve or maintain the good and just society because it is the origin of both our biological and moral selves.

The family then is a basic unit of society, and as such is part of a larger unit, be it neighborhood, village, city, nation, or humanity. The family helps to establish the fact that we are by nature social and that we are as individuals bonded together into social wholes or societies that are more than organic or biological units.

You and I are Sullivans, Roman Catholics, Bostonians, Americans, and Westerners. "Family" points to our basic unit of origin and procreation but it can also stand for much which has little direct relation to origin, creation, and natural bondedness. There is a great difference between our membership in a family of origin and procreation and our membership in many another close, warm, intimate and organic association of persons.

When I visit the church of my youth, I find there many persons who nurtured, loved, and supported me throughout much of my life. They share with me many experiences of anxiety, sorrow, and happiness. They have introduced me to other adults and children whom I did not know and who, in turn, helped to form me and my world. Their care, comfort, and presence cause me to think of the congregation as family, as a vital part of who I am. Yet, when I use the term "family" in relation to them, I know that it is by extension. Care, warmth, intimacy, and trust inclines me both to call them family and to recognize that in significant and crucial ways they are not family. The family of origin and procreation shares with other human associations qualities, values, and relationships thought frequently to be peculiar to the biological family. While in most instances we are quite clear in distinguishing these other human associations from the family of origin and procreation, we sometimes conflate the term "family" to include those social units that are family by analogy. This often occurs when we speak of the family as the foundation of society or the fundamental unit of society. It is important however, for us to remember that while the family is a basic unit of society, it also shares many of its qualities and values with other units smaller and larger than itself but no less essential. This is most clear when we speak of home, church, and school, the basic institutions which nurture the individual and transmit to him or her the general culture of humankind. By viewing family in the context of society, we are made more aware of our usage of the term both to designate a biological unit and to point to types of human bondedness we think peculiar to or best developed within that biological unit.

We would not be as much concerned with families, culture, or ethics as we are today if they were not bound together in the fate of a particular society. We would be less concerned with this topic if there were no common society in which these institutions existed and in which the nature and functioning of the family affected and was affected by the vital institutions of that society, such as its religious, educational, economic, governmental and legal institutions. Because the rules and roles shared by the family, culture, and ethics are embedded in the society of the United States of America during the decades of the 80s and 90s, they take on for us great significance. What focuses attention on the family and what is at stake is the nature of the society at this historical juncture and in the future. I am concerned not to neglect the unique and distinctive importance and nature of the family, but I do believe that that uniqueness can be properly understood only in the context of the society in which the family is embedded.

Culture, like family, does not float free; it too is located in a society or related to institutions, groups, and individuals whose patterns of interaction are relatively fixed by roles and rules. Culture tends to determine or at least to influence that basic social unit, the family, so that people come to understand it to be monogamous, polygamous, nuclear, extended patriarchal or matriarchal. While most contemporary Christians might describe the family as monogamous and nuclear, that picture of the family by no means goes unchallenged by Scripture, tradition, history, or human experience, and in most instances, the differences among these conceptions of family has to do with culture and not with place or status in society. Culture, then, is important. As a collection of values and beliefs it helps to shape, often in determinative ways, the structure and function of the family, and like the family, it is itself influenced by the nature of the society in which it exists. The American society is an excellent example. The many immigrant groups that have come to this nation have sought to preserve their former family structures, customs, and traditions. They have made efforts to isolate themselves in neighborhoods, to build elaborate exclusive lodges and cultural institutions, and to control the marriage practices of their children. They have called themselves by two names in order to keep loyalties and obligations alive. Yet the American culture and the immigrants' interactions with the other peoples of Great Britain, Europe, Africa, and Asia has altered significantly the family structures of all these groups. The Second Vatican Council indicates that these cultural forces are so powerful that they demand changes, up-dating, even on the part of a church dedicated to continuity of norms and practices. Moreover, the great social and political movements taking place in today's world, in Iran, among the ethnic sub-groups of the Soviet Union, in Cambodia and China, indicate again how cultural changes influence the formation of families. Cultural forces are so great that at least one cultural observer believes all the world will become the West, and fundamentalists of many religious groups envision a return to a religiously pure past age. The knowledge of the influence of culture upon the family is so firm and widespread that both nations and religious associations have been willing over the centuries to commit large portions of their resources to ensure the continuance of certain desired structures of belief and action in that institution. The family may be basic but it does not determine society, culture, or ethic.

Ethics, like family and culture, is also very diverse and very complex. Although ethics today is quite frequently spoken of as if it were some magic elixir that can quickly and without conflict sort out what is mine and what is thine, what is good and what is evil, and what is right and what is wrong, it too, we must remember, is no less ambiguous and unclear than are our conceptions of family and culture. Like these other conceptions, it too is related to something outside itself, to society and culture, to self and selves in relation to other selves, including the family. When we relate ethics then to family and culture, we must be aware of its embeddedness in a specific society as well as in particular cultures and families. Since it is our habit to think of family and culture in concrete and particular ways, and since it is the desire of our day to correct the evils of class, race, and sex discrimination, it is of great importance that we be sensitive to the limited and parochial traditions in which our moral thinking is rooted. This is necessary especially when we are speaking in ways which are considered universal and transcendent. When we say for example, "a constructive ethic will require that we can distance ourselves from our family, culture, and society and by an effort of thought and imagination understand the claims of others and properly consider them in relation to the claims made by ourselves and by those with special relationships to us," we need to be aware of the fact that we are employing a Western, American, Christian rational mode of moral reasoning. Some Americans and many people of other cultures will not share our belief that we are being sufficiently critical and impartial. They will perceive distortions in our moral reasoning. It is important to acknowledge then contemporary society equates ethics with the functioning of so-called blue-ribbon committees whose missions are to restore customary Western conceptions of harmony and peace rather than discover and implement justice. If we are wont to trumpet our traditions, our interests, our special relationships and loyalties, then it is important that we acknowledge the partiality in moral reasoning. Having discovered our lack of a holistic and universal vision in ethics, we should be more rather than less reticent to impose it on others.

Family, culture, and ethics are indeed broad and comprehensive terms. They are, however, interrelated and joined together by a conception of society in which the cultural values and beliefs will greatly influence the moral rules and norms which will determine the structure and functioning of the family. One can conclude in addition that none of these terms are understood by us as abstractions. They are all laden with history, Western, Christian, and American history. Our sense of these concepts and institutions are greatly influenced also by where we are located in this history and how we understand it. For most of us, the understanding of these terms are greatly affected by the twentieth century American society with its units of home and workplace, work and leisure, white-collar and blue-collar, male and female, public and private, white, black, Hispanic, and Asian, and its great anxiety about how to deal with the issues arising from these divisions of society and the strains associated with them. This then is the context in which we are to consider the topic of family, culture, and ethics. How do we begin? What can we say?

The proper place of beginning is with the culture of a society, even if we grant that the family is a basic unit. This is because the family *qua* family is a relationship of blood, a biological unit. The rights, duties, and meanings associated with the family are cultural and do not proceed independently from the genes or behavior of single families. Moreover, they will vary according to culture. If we speak thus of a Catholic or Protestant culture or ethic, we seek to convey the idea that a particular ethos determines to a considerable degree the nature of the family. If we ask how Catholicism or Protestantism and their cultures came to be, few if any of us would talk about families and their stabilities or even of the conversions of families. We are more apt to speak of ideas, of individuals, of social movements, or national societies. The structure and functioning of the family is derivative from the culture of a larger society or the bonding of individuals who possess a specific ideological, religious, or national understanding. The family is not basic because it is the primary institution but because it is the institution through which societies, associations, or communities reproduce themselves and maintain their cultural patterns. We in America are becoming increasingly aware of and concerned about the family not because we care so much about family *qua* family but because we, or at least many of us, are greatly concerned about the changes that are taking place in our economic, social, religious, and political institutions. We desire to maintain cultural patterns that are for some in the society very meaningful or which are seen as more conducive for human flourishing than the emerging new cultural forms. In America during our time, there is a great sense of urgency about what is to be preserved and passed on to future generations and a great sense of anxiety about innovations in societal institutions. The reasons for this are multiple, but one important cause is the collapse of the hegemony of the dominant Protestant culture and the aggressive attempts of other cultures—Roman Catholic, Jewish, humanist, black, feminist—to imprint in a permanent way the changing American culture. In addition, there is the pressure stemming from economic and technological change, a new wave of immigrants, and the explosion of knowledge and communication concerning ourselves and our world. All of these factors and many more effect in significant ways how we bond ourselves with others, what we seek to inculcate into those with whom we are bonded, and what we shall attempt to maintain and keep alive in our shared life. The demands that both liberal and conservative Americans have set for themselves, namely to direct if not engineer the culture, is an exceedingly complex and difficult demand. More daunting than the task John Winthrop accepted when he spoke to his companions, largely of one race, class, religion, and nationality, on the *Arabelle* on their way to the city set upon a hill. More complex also than the task created by the problem of loss experienced by the successive waves of immigrants, largely of one race, class and religion, that came to these shores. Perhaps of all Americans, only the African Americans faced a more difficult task because they experienced not only the loss of homeland and severe cultural disruption that was experienced by European peoples but, upon their arrival on these shores, they also had their families systematically and deliberately destroyed by the white colonist. The social institution entrusted with the task of socialization, nurturance, and memory was destroyed in order to furnish white families with labor and leisure. Under the most restricted of conditions, which did not encourage or aid permanent bonding and which took from the laborers the fruit of their labor and the opportunity to be responsible for their own lives and to contribute to their heirs an accumulation of culture and wealth, the African Americans had to forge a new culture and sustain societal life without either a complete or stable family and without full access to the new and foreign culture into which they were placed. How different the lives of the African Americans might have been had they been able to keep the property they created by mixing their labor with it, or had they been permitted full access to the cultural and societal institutions of the United States, or had they been able to maintain their families and their conceptions of legitimacy, even an ordered, responsible polygamy.

Culture is an important force in family formation and it is in part because of America's positive reinforcement of white families and negative actions toward African American families that the former families enjoy a societal advantage. In spite of certain unfairnesses toward some white ethnic and religious groups, America bestowed upon European and British immigrants a greater vision and opportunity for self-realization than they had enjoyed in their lands of origin. This together with the natural resources of the continent enabled them to improve their status and position. Family structure and ethic did not alone create the success of America. The Mormons represent a conspicuous example of how a non-normative family structure and ethic did not greatly impede economic success—

provided a supportive cultural matrix was present. On the other hand, the persistently negative attitude and policies toward African Americans and the American Indians present in the American culture demonstrate how a hostile environment can prevent or destroy achievement in all of life, including the family. The destruction of native peoples and their family cannot be set forth here. We must record, however, that a hostile negative attitude and set of policies were adopted toward them soon after the first encounters and, in spite of much improvement, persists today. These cultural attitudes and policies are to a great extent responsible for their present plight. Any policy or program designed to create a healthier and more whole family policy must be rooted thus in efforts to create a healthier and more whole culture. The expanded opportunity the American nation presented to white families at the time of the nation's formation and during the period of its massive industrial growth was in effect a governmental policy supportive of family. This national policy provided land, jobs, education, political power, aid for home purchases, and access to financial institutions. From this, African Americans were largely excluded. The hostile American culture of neglect and discrimination deformed them as a people and as families. This process continues today and can be documented in respect to religion, education, housing, law, employment, and financial institutions. Consequently, our task today, if we care as a people to improve the family and our national ethic, is to strengthen our effort to make culture and society more just and good. The Roman Catholic Church is a hierarchical institution that seeks, through cultural teaching, doctrine, and morals, to teach families how to make wise choices and enhance their lives. The church does not remain silent in respect to the evil in culture and society while condemning every personal evil present among individuals and families. Nor does it, without any assistance from its resources of money, programs, and faith, instruct the unhealthy to heal themselves. What the church has come to recognize as unwise, many Americans have adopted as an adequate family policy. They deny the dominant role of culture in family formation and destruction and they demand that isolated and socially disadvantaged families heal themselves. Such a program and cultural attitude makes exceedingly difficult the creation of healthy and whole families, and its influence upon the masses cannot be overcome by the heroic achievement of a few individuals and families. Even though we must acknowledge our inability to accurately and precisely engineer cultural change, we must nevertheless recognize that any major flaw in family structure and functioning most likely has its origin in a cultural flaw and is transmitted to families and through families by cultural values and institutions. It is usually the rich, the powerful, or the well-educated who legitimate deviant patterns of thought and action and the poor, the weak, or the less educated who experience the pathology. LSD, marijuana, and cocaine use among the upper classes prepared the way for the widespread drug abuse found today among the lower classes. Any effort to improve the family must be accompanied by an effort to improve the culture, for our best knowledge informs us that the source of the ailment to the family is to be found in the culture.

A statement about the relationship of black and white families can serve to illustrate my point. Much is said in our day about the gap between the white and black family with respect to income, health, crime, and education. In explaining the gap, every effort is made not to refer to racial discrimination by white persons or institutions. Anti-Semitism may be seen as having its origins in the New Testament of the Christian Scriptures and as persisting still in our society which is more just to Jewish persons than any other society except Israel. Class differences may be traced to the ancient world and the origins of capitalism and be seen to persist still today. Similarly with patriarchy. Yet, we have been told, racism and racial discrimination in a nation established as half-slave and half-free, has been so fully eradicated that in less than 30 years there exists within the black family and community no identifiable or disabling legacies of slavery, legalized segregation or unjust discrimination. Moreover, this miracle was accomplished without the full enforcement of existing civil rights legislation or the passage of any major new pieces of legislation, and during a period when the nation's attention and resources were severely strained by the war in Vietnam, the resignation of a president, the fall of the economy from its place of world leadership and an eight-year attack upon racial equality led by President Reagan. In addition, our domestic tranquility was disrupted by controversies in respect to women's rights, entitlement programs for the poor, abortion, Central American foreign policy, fundamentalism, drug abuse and much else. In spite of all these happenings in our society, which slowed down or stopped actions to mitigate racism, the present tendency is to extol whites for their fairness and to blame the black family for the increasing gap between the white and black family.

Alexis de Tocqueville, in his oft-quoted *Democracy in America,* had these words to say about the African-American family: "The Negro has no family: woman is merely the temporary companion of his pleasures, and his children are on an equality with himself from the moment of their birth."[1] The white colonist in America, like those in the Caribbean and those in present-day South Africa, acted in a systematic and deliberate manner to destroy the black family. The tyranny of the laws and the intolerance of the people created for African Americans a reality not experienced by any other group in America. Moreover, the indifference or the repugnance of the white population for African Americans has meant that the United States' government has never devised a federal program to aid black families in the manner that it has aided and supported white families and some of the recent immigrants. The work of W.E.B. Du-Bois and E. Franklin Frazier, as well as the chapters on the Negro family in Myrdal's *American Dilemma* contain this conclusion and were intended to call the larger society's attention to its destructive policies toward the black family.[2] But then, as now, that message has not been heard. During slavery there was a group of African Americans and a few whites who struggled, and on occasion successfully, to establish the black family. Similar action took place during Reconstruction and in every other period of American history. Frazier wrote during the period of the New Deal when, in spite of Hitler's racism in Europe, United States' policies to aid white families systematically excluded African Americans from similar benefits in housing, education, health care, and work. During the period from emancipation to the end of World War II, blacks struggled to overcome slavery's destruction of the family, but while a few survived, the majority of the community was unable to acquire the resources needed to overcome their exclusion from the opportunity systems in both the North and the South. The blame rested not alone with the black family; it rested also as Myrdal indicated, and later Winthrop Jordan in his volume *White Over Black*,[3] with the cultural values of American society. The claim that these cultural values and this history have been significantly altered and that opportunity systems are equally open to all races in America is simply not true.

The cultural values which have resulted in the perpetuation of a distorted or incomplete African-American family are still present among blacks. They are carried by white personal and institutional racism and by the black subculture. To the extent that black subculture carries the distortions introduced by slavery, blacks can be blamed for their social location, but fairness demands some assumption of responsibility on the part of the larger society for the instillation of these values among blacks and the withholding from blacks of the opportunities and resources needed to overcome these hindrances once they had been implanted and allowed to grow. De Tocqueville informs us that for more than 250 years America encouraged, indeed compelled, teenage pregnancy, out-of-wedlock birth, absent fathers and dependency among African Americans, and discouraged by all means monogamous nuclear families. If Charles Murray finds this to be the welfare policy of the 60s and 70s we can only conclude that nothing has changed.[4] Murray's error consists only in explaining a historical and widespread public policy by reference to recent legislative acts and their alleged consequences.

Some scholars are willing to accept what I have said in respect to the slave-holding South but deny its validity in respect to the North or to the period since emancipation, especially the last 30 years. I cannot in this brief paper state fully my argument for cultural continuity. Evidence for continuity can be provided in abundance by an investigation of African American folklore, the records of black migration to southern and northern cities, the blues and the secular song tradition, and sociological studies such as those of DuBois and Frazier. Since this assault upon the African American family took place throughout the Americas, the migration of blacks from the other regions such as the Caribbean increased the number of unstable and single-parent families.

My point, then, is this. The gap between the white and black family in America is to a great extent the result of the destruction of the black family during slavery and the continuation of racist values inimical to the black family in the American cultural system. This is one of many illustrations of how cultural values determine in large measure the nature of the family and not the family the culture. The interstices in the value system and the determination of some black individuals has throughout the history of the United States resulted in the creation of some strong and whole black families, but even where this has happened the racism present in the economic, educational, and housing institutions has prevented the rapid growth of the nuclear or mainstream African-American family. If it is true that cultural deficits contribute to and cause the creation of unhealthy families, then it follows that one avenue to the improvement of family is through the creation of a more adequate ethic. Most studies of the American family which have explicitly or implicitly spoken about family ethics have tended to assume the middle-class white family to be normative and all other families, especially the African-American family, to be disorganized and pathological. Gunnar Myrdal's *The American Dilemma* and Daniel P. Moynihan's *The Negro American Family* are two illustrations of this popular and widespread approach.[5] Although the social scientist may begin with the intention of carrying out a descriptive and factual study and of making the society more aware of its injustices to some portion of the community, most frequently the black community, the results of the study often portray the nonwhite middle-class family as pathological and lead some to conclude that this is due to the fact that nonwhite middle-class families are lacking in an adequate amount of moral characteristics. They then are to be blamed for their social status and location rather than the dominant societies' cultural values and policy choices. Social scientists cannot and must not be blamed for the usages to which their studies are put, but they are in some sense accountable. This is why I have selected the Myrdal study and the Moynihan report. The former represents a more adequate approach to ethics.

Today many social scientists, government policy-makers and moralists have decried the existence in our society of female-headed households. These households are censured because they are associated with poverty and are believed to be a major cause of poverty in African-American families and in racial-ethnic communities. In addition, these households are often morally criticized because many of them are the result of out-of-wedlock teenage births. Since many of these households are formed in the African-American community, that community is stigmatized, or rather its stigmatization is further legitimated by reference to these births. The consequence is the blaming of the black community for the gap between white and black income and employment and the advocacy of self-help as a public policy cure. Moynihan once called it "benign neglect." A kind of family ethic which sees much of the cure to poverty, crime, illegitimacy, illness, and unemployment in intervention in the black family has become the focus for social and cultural betterment.

It would be unwise for any black or white individual to attempt to deny the facts about African-American poverty, crime, or sexuality. Black or white individuals who do so should be criticized for being socially and morally irresponsible and in error. At the same time, the social scientist, policy-maker, and moralist who suggests, without clear and forcefully-stated qualifications, that the more privileged status of the middle-class white family is due to merit or superior ethical behavior is also to be criticized. One important difference between Myrdal's *American Dilemma* and Moynihan's report is the attention paid to creation of an ethic for the family. Myrdal examines the values of the culture and attempts to develop an ethic based upon its highest ideals and applicable to all its people equally. Moynihan, however, accepts the white middle-class family as normative and understands their achievements in the light of his own interpretation of his religious community's social teaching, and then measures the African-American family against this norm. Whatever his intentions, his procedure was morally defective and no one should have been surprised by their fueling of the belief that the African-American family, not the culture and society, was the most important source of its own ill-fortune and that white families were moral exemplars. The failure of Moynihan and others to state in an unambiguous and straightforward manner how the cultural values of the American society contributes to the poverty associated with female-headed households has obscured the nature of family ethics and confused the understanding of the poverty problem. The issue is not whether a large number of black and white teenagers have given birth to children out of wedlock, but rather how one assesses the social and personal moral responsibility for those actions which are generally considered unacceptable by both blacks and whites. By misunderstanding the relationship between culture and family and between ethics and the social practices of the dominant groups in society, Moynihan and some others have confused the role of ethics in family structure and functioning.

Just as culture tends to determine family structure and functioning, it also tends to influence an individual's judgment about right and wrong, good and bad. While a complete separation of cultural and ethical norms may be impossible, it is important that we seek to do just that and that we be constantly self-critical in this respect. This is especially important in a society like the American one where cultural judgments are biased in favor of white middle-class persons and Western Christian and humanistic values. Moynihan did not do this in his report on the Negro family. He assumed his own religious and moral values to be absolute, accepted as normative the values of a society which he freely admitted was biased in respect to white patriarchy, and sought to impose upon the African-American family his perception of what their family ought to be. The procedure he followed, even if it were motivated by good intentions, was not oriented to the discovery of moral truth about either society, culture, or family. It is a method one must not follow in seeking to relate these institutions or to discover their true nature.

Max Weber demonstrated for many the fact that cultures tend to produce distinctive ethics. This was true not only for Protestant and Catholics but also for the adherents to Judaism and the religions of China and India. The ethic of families was shown to have been derived from a culture. Since a culture like that of America has been enriched by the coming together of many cultures, the ethics found among the families will vary and families within this multicultural society will be open to the influences of several cultures other than their own. Consequently, there will always be possibilities open for choice, but choices largely from options present in the American society. Transcendence of this culture, while possible, will require considerable effort and moral tenacity. In such a setting it is perhaps not honest or right to suggest that the least-advantaged members of a society are fully responsible for all their moral failures and that social policy should be designed to punish them more harshly than the advantaged. Since the actual openness of choice available to each family will depend upon a host of factors such as intelligence, education, exposure to cultural experiences, and the possession of resources for the implementation of choices, account should be taken of the restricted nature of choice available to the least advantaged. A proper approach to a family ethic will therefore follow a procedure like that of Gunnar Myrdal, which made an effort to create an objective norm based upon an evaluation of the normative understandings of the total American people and ideals. This sort of procedure will not by itself rid one of all traces of relativism or partiality to Western and European-dominated ethical norms, but it ought to alert sensitive and fair-minded people to the fact that all persons and groups ought not to be held similarly accountable without any attempt being made to discover how their choices have been narrowed by cultural and societal factors, especially those generated by social policymakers. While in the final analysis the family in a sense makes the choice, one needs to recognize fully the cultural limitations of that choice. Protestants are inclined to be persuaded by Protestant moral reasoning and Catholics by Catholic moral reasoning. Normally, we do not expect a Protestant family ethic to flourish in Rome or a Catholic family ethic to flourish in Tibet. Such may, of course, occur, but if it does we look for some special conditions to explain the happening. Whether, then, an ethic is autonomous, heteronomous, or theonomous, it is to a great extent shaped by the culture and its location within the culture. Critical reflection on the ethics of families needs to keep this in mind.

Such reflection must not assume that the nuclear middle-class family possesses the best family ethic simply because it mirrors more fully the cultural expectations for a family or that the one-parent or some other form of the family lacks moral integrity because its cultural form is not the preferred one. One might argue, as I began to do earlier, that the single teenage mother, the one-parent family, and the father-absent family were deliberately created by white Americans during the period of slavery and have been maintained by American racism, sexism, and patriarchy, as well as by persons within the African-American sub-culture, and that the solution to these problems requires an adjustment of societal and cultural values, change in the nature and functioning of all American families and the elimination of racism and sexism. Such an approach would assert that families have a responsibility to be self-critical and culturally critical in choosing their ethic. It would recognize that many individuals and families considered to be pathological were least able to overcome the social obstacles that encumbered them, such as poor verbal skills and schooling, inadequate income, limited experience, and psychological deficiencies that make them unable to undertake the needed programs of correction in respect to cultural value orientations. Indeed, they are often the ones most vulnerable to succumbing to the evils present in the society, and disproportionately in their own communities and perhaps families. On the other hand, those families most favored by the prevailing establishment ethic and used by Moynihan to establish the norms, contain among themselves the middle-class families which Robert Bellah and Steven Tipton and the other authors of *Habits of the Heart* contend are unable to think in moral categories.[6] If this is true, then we and many a social scientist and policymaker need to reexamine our usage of the terms "normative" and "pathological" in respect to the American family.

It is important, therefore, to recognize that a cultural or familial ethic is often skewed by cultural considerations. It is not enough to decide what is right or wrong upon the basis of its contribution to cultural or family stability or even to black/white parity in family income.

An examination of the last of our three institutions, the family, makes it clear that one cannot affirm without a great deal of straightforward qualifications that the family is the fundamental social institution and that it is able, without assistance from the larger society, to develop adequately and to create a just and good community. The family is certainly a basic social institution and it does help to determine the health and virtue of society, but neither its structure nor its functioning is unaffected by the culture and the ethic it sanctions. The high rate of teenage births and the increasing decision of never-married, middle-class white women not to have children indicates that homes are going to be formed without a father being present. New forms of the family are destined to exist alongside the traditional family, even though they may require redefinition of legitimacy and morality. Moreover, the traditional family, already modified by the high rate of divorce and remarriage, will undergo even further change because of the increasing tendency of mothers to enter the work force and to insist that the roles of breadwinner, homemaker and child-rearer be shared by both spouses. Changes in the nature of sexual practices, women's conception of themselves and their roles, and the economic work place are bringing about changes in the nature of family structure and functioning. The traditional nuclear family or extended family can no longer be said to be normative. The family structure thought to have been pathological is now widespread and accepted, and the function felt by many to have been fixed by nature or God or both are being seen as cultural creations subject to change by the men and women who fulfill them. Nurturance is seen to depend more on love, affection, financial resources, and intelligence than the presence of two parents of differing sex. The concern of the society and Senator Moynihan has shifted from the female-headed family and absent father to the mother working outside of the home and the securing of child support payments from the father of the child. The white middle-class nuclear family is no longer normative and even some of its most dogmatic supporters are willing to acknowledge that the American family has undergone structural and functional change. With an ever-larger percentage of parents working in order to sustain a high standard of living, and many women insisting that they have the right to pursue a vocation outside the home and be financially independent and that their husbands become housekeepers and homemakers, the family more and more resembles a social union of individuals determined by cultural convictions than a natural unit determined by biological differences and heavenly choices. The seriousness of these changes is symbolized by the willingness of some within Christian and Jewish religious associations to cease symbolizing God as Father. This change alters the nature of authority the male can claim for his place in the family and frees the responsibilities of the spouses from gender determination. Nurturance can now be shared by the spouses as they think feasible and best, and since they are, broadly speaking, human qualities rather than motherly or fatherly ones, they can more easily be provided by institutions and persons outside the home such as child day-care centers, educational clubs, programs, schools, and recreational and religious associations. Since in our society most of these nurturing institutions are private and charge a fee, those with little money have fewer such services available to aid them to cope with the changes in the family resulting from cultural and economic changes in the society.

These changes in the family which have taken place in the last 30 years are another indicator of the fact that the family is not self-sufficient and capable of determining the nature of the culture or its ethic. The family is rather one of several basic societal institutions and is determined to a considerable extent by its cultural matrix. If one does, as did Patrick J. Moynihan in his report on the Negro family, take the white middle-class family as a normative model for the family, then what is termed pathology has undergone great change and needs to be seen in the light of cultural relativism and not some conception of natural law. The experience of the last 30 years suggests that the problem is not simply the female-headed household or the absent father, but also the lack of financial resources and the availability of institutions which can provide emotional and psychological support. One may note also that Myrdal's procedure remains better suited for constructing an ethic because its norms, equality and justice, remain stable even though their content must be reformed because of the change in family structure and function.

The concern of gays and lesbians to form families is perhaps the most radical development in respect to the restructuring of the family because it tends to eliminate the function of procreation and to envision the family as an exclusively child-rearing and care-giving institution. While a cultural consensus has not yet developed giving considerable approval to this understanding of the family, this challenge to rethink family is important for illustrating again how cultural and ethical changes affect the conception of the family and how the traditional family undergoes reformulation. The shifting nature of the definition of the family points to the fact that the family is but one of the fundamental and basic institutions of the society.

The changing nature of the family has some saliency for understanding the changes taking place in the African-American family and the view of some in respect to those new patterns. The shifting structure and function of the American family points to the importance of culture as well as family or individual choice in family formation. It is my belief that the more flexible cultural understanding of the family has led to a greater acceptance of formerly deviant forms of association. Some of the pathology resulting from the vulnerability of the African-American to destructive social conditions, such as urbanization, inferior housing, poor education, economic dislocation, and the lack of private and public resources, has been made to appear acceptable because of Woodstock and the so-called permissive society of the 60's and 70's. The popular nature of these events and the isolation of many African-Americans from the other aspects of culture made the community more willing to accept their own practices and helped to further undermine traditional conceptions of the family which, because of history and racism, were already weak among many in this racial-ethnic society. Forces which may have been helpful in loosening a too-rigid ethic in middle-class white America became life-threatening in this community, where resistance was slight. Whatever the errors of judgment, the ability to establish a whole and healthy, though different, family has not vanished. Indeed, some interpreters felt that the riots of the 60's and 70's were cries of help and that the new concerns of the small but growing black middle class for the family is an important movement in the direction of healing and restoral. Be that as it may, we need only to recognize that the African-American family is not the only non-traditional family and its blameworthiness should be assessed in a fashion comparable to the evaluations made of similar white middle-class families. Put a bit differently, we might say that in the last quarter-century, social and cultural changes have given more support to the change of family structure and functioning than to the maintenance of the traditional nuclear structure. In the process, the already weak African-American family was greatly damaged because it did not have the resources and strength needed to manage change. Our current concern with children rearing children would be less great if the children who are parents were not poor, uneducated, and unrelated to a wide range of health and social support services. Cultural changes and social location have speeded the erosion of traditional family values and patterns among African-Americans. The process of family reorganization is widespread throughout the society and should be treated as a national problem, but within our society slavery and racism have made a special case of the African-American. This special case requires special attention to its needs.

The investigation undertaken in this paper concerning the relation of culture, ethic, and family to each other indicates that all these social institutions play an important part in the creation and maintenance of a just and good society, and that while the family may be thought of as the basic institution in society, its structure, function, and ethic is to a considerable degree shaped by the culture of the society in which it is rooted. A remaking of the family determined by what is needed to achieve success in a particular society, even one as well structured as the American society, while important, will in most instances not lead to either an adequate ethic or a whole and healthy society. This is due to the fact that family, like culture, is often harmful to some of its constituents and to others at the same time that it experiences some success. The very qualities, such as trust, love, and mutual caring, which make for bondedness and equality among family members can develop loyalties which are not shared with those outside the family. Our references to the African-American families help to make this clear because the larger American society has developed cultural and ethical values which make it extremely difficult for white or African-American families to see that they are members of a common family or people, in spite of their shared nationality and frequently Christian faith. The notion of a good family does not entail communal bondedness and supportiveness. There is a familial atomism that sets family against family and perpetuates social divisions. The special relationships generated in the family weaken the ability of the family to engage in the creation of a just and fair society or common good. Only if the insights embodied in this paper, namely that a good family are the product of a good culture as well as personal virtue, are appropriated by the ethic will justice be enlarged. Any proper construction of a family, an ethic, a culture, and a society must be aware of the extent to which the achievements of a family are limited by social and cultural factors. Since no family able to create fully its own ethic and the ability to fulfill all its imperatives, the transformation of family and culture must be addressed by forces beyond that of the family. The ethic that is required is a social ethic fashioned by the modifications of its special relationships and the development of its interactions with other families. This will include honest endeavors to treat others as it treats its own members. The adequate family ethic will not tell other families to be like us but will aggressively act to secure the good life for those not a member of its intimate group. It must not seek to maximize its good at the expense of others. It will seek to create loyalties that reach beyond family and embrace all members of society. Such an ethic will undertake to love the neighbor as the self and to love God more than father, mother, or children.

It has long been recognized that one of the grave errors of a family ethic is nepotism, the preference for one's own family even when that preference cannot be justified as fair. We cannot in the name of social or family stability accept and recommend these forms of greed. The proper family ethic must be a just and loving social ethic, and that means identification of and reliance upon cultural values and institutions that manifest these characteristics.

The social nature of the family ethic should not, however, detract from the obligation to honor special relationships. It should rather put them in proper relation to those responsibilities we owe others. Families need to be concerned for the common good, relationship between states, the sustaining of the earth and the continuation of the species. They should recognize also that the families that assume and fulfill these moral obligations can be various in form. Jesse Jackson, Daniel Patrick Moynihan, and W. E. B. DuBois are products of father-absent or mother-only families. Some crime families, on the other hand, are excellent illustrations of the possible moral impotence of a stable nuclear family where love and material goods are amply showered upon family members without regard to social responsibility. The proper family ethic, then, must be a balancing of love and care from members for each other, together with a concern to work diligently and persistently and in solidarity with others on behalf of the common good. Recognition of the ability of all forms of family to make constructive contributions to the common good will aid us to see the beneficial aspects of a society in which many, not one, forms of family structure exist.

Notes

1. De Tocqueville, Alexis, *Democracy in America* (New York: Alfred A. Knopf, 1957) Vol. I 332.

2. Rainwater, Lee and W. L. Yancy, *The Moynihan Report and the Politics of Controversy* (Cambridge, MA: M.I.T., 1967); Frazier, E. Franklin, *The Negro Family in the United States*, rev. and abridged ed. (Chicago: University of Chicago, 1966); Myrdal, Gunnar, *An American Dilemma* (New York: Harper & Row, 1962).

3. Jordan, Winthrop, *White Over Black* (Baltimore: Penguin Books, 1969).

4. Murray, Charles, *Losing Ground* (New York: Basic Books, 1984).

5. Moynihan, Daniel Patrick, *Family and Nation* (New York: Harcourt Brace Jovanovich, 1986).

6. Bellah, Robert N., Richard N. Madsen, William M. Sullivan, Ann Swidler and Steven M. Tipton, *Habits of the Heart: Individualism and Commitment in American Life* (Berkeley, University of California, 1985).

Family Rights and Public Policy

Richard A. McCormick, S.J.
University of Notre Dame

I have always been intrigued by an apparent anomaly within the Catholic community. On the one hand, there has been a steady flow of documents beginning with *Rerum novarum* and continuing through *Quadragesimo anno, Pacem in terris, Populorum progressio, Octogesima adveniens, Laborem exercens* and *Sollicitudo rei socialis*. On the other hand, there has coexisted with these a kind of dormant social conscience within rank and file Catholicism. There are any number of possible explanations for this that need not detain us long here. The simplest is, as Sr. Thea Bowman pointed out to the American bishops at Seton Hall on June 17, 1989, that though the Church has excellent documents, nobody reads them.[1] Or again, one could make a plausible case for arguing that, notwithstanding documents like the ones mentioned above, organized Catholicism still managed to convey—indeed, exude—the idea that its real interests, where it will "fight for the right without question or pause," lie elsewhere (birth control, celibacy, ordination of women, etc.) Eugene Kennedy's *recent* book, *Tomorrow's Catholics, Yesterday's Church*, would make such a point.[2]

Whatever the case, a similar fate has met the Charter of Family Rights. The Synod of 1980 contained calls for such a charter. In *Familiaris consortio* (1981), John Paul II listed some rights mentioned by the synod fathers and promised a document from the Holy See. On October 22, 1983, the Charter on the Rights of the Family appeared.[3] I am not being facetious when I say that it disappeared in 1983. Very little has been heard of this Charter since then. I do not see it cited in the literature, quoted in public fora, leaned on in desperate situations or functioning in legislative overtures. In brief, it is not an exaggeration to say that it is a dead and forgotten document. That is regrettable.

For this reason I want to take the most unusual step of enclosing this document *in toto* in this chapter as its final footnote. Furthermore, it should be read at this point, because my subsequent remarks suppose familiarity with the document. Attempts to adumbrate the Charter are doomed to failure, given the crucial importance of qualifying details and proposals.

Several notes are in place here about this Charter. First, the Charter's listing represents a rather obvious effort to state rights in such a way that they remain valid in spite of variation of culture. For instance, when discussing the "free and full consent of the spouses" (n. 2), the Charter notes: "With due respect for the traditional role of the families in certain cultures in guiding the decision of their children, all pressure . . . is to be avoided." Yet, a case can be made for concluding that the Charter did not always succeed here. For instance, under n. 5 it states: "The rights of parents are violated when a compulsory system of education is imposed by the State from which all religious formation is excluded." How would such a statement fare in a country that understands and honors separation of church and state as we do in the United States?

A similar question might be raised under n. 3. The Charter asserts: "The activities of public authorities and private organizations which attempt in any way to limit the freedom of couples in deciding about their children constitute a grave offense against human dignity and justice." That "in any way" is sweeping. Is parental freedom *absolute*? Is it *totally* unrelated to the social setting in which it is exercised? Do governments have no rights and responsibilities if spousal freedom is exacerbating a genuine population problem? One need not agree with specific policies in China to believe that the Charter's statement falls into the category of *prima facie* obligations only in that country. I shall return to this point below.

A second point: the rights listed are understood as rooted in the natural law, "that law which is inscribed by the Creator in the heart of every human being." The listing, therefore, is not a Catholic one, but a catholic one. Christian revelation does not originate these rights; rather, it enlightens the natural reality of the family.

Third, these rights are presented in a charter. I confess that it is not totally clear to me what the document means by this. It attempts to clarify the notion by stating what a charter is not. It is not an exposition of the moral theology of the family, "although it reflects the Church's thinking in the matter." Nor is it a "code of conduct for persons or institutions." Finally, the Charter is "different from a simple declaration of theoretical principles concerning the family."

More positively, the Charter states that it aims to formulate "the fundamental rights that are inherent in that natural and universal society which is the family." In spite of these qualifications, the specific character of a charter remains obscure.

Fourth, the Charter "is addressed principally to governments". Thus, it should function "as a model and a point of reference for the drawing up of legislation and family policy." But the Charter is also addressed to intergovernmental international organizations, to families, and to all men and women.

The above four points are drawn from the statements of the Charter itself. This is the place to raise some general questions about rights not addressed in this Charter, but, I believe, provoked by it and essential to understanding it. These general questions were raised several years ago by John Langan, S.J.[4]

One such question concerns the weight to be accorded to human rights in moral and political argument. Do rights' claims have priority over other considerations? Langan believes that rights' claims have a kind of *"prima facie* status" which puts the burden of justification on those proposing to override these claims. Correspondingly, this understanding affirms a *prima facie* obligation on others to satisfy such claims. As Langan concludes:

> The point to bear in mind is that human rights have both a presumption of priority, which requires that infringements be justified by morally acceptable reasons, and a graduated urgency corresponding to the varying importance and necessity of the values that they protect.[5]

The Charter discusses neither a "graduated urgency" nor the matter of the absoluteness of rights.

Another important point not discussed in the Charter but raised by it is the difference between personal and political rights, and social and economic rights. Under social and economic rights are claims to social security, work, education, food, clothing, housing, etc. These are positive rights in the sense that they can only be satisfied by supplying the goods in question. Because the ability to provide such goods depends on a society's wealth and because many societies are too poor to do so, some commentators are reluctant to speak of claims to these goods as rights—especially if they regard human rights as exceptionless. The Charter lumps together, indiscriminately, political-personal rights and social-economic rights. The consequences of this could be alarming. The most immediate consequence is to confuse, and to some extent to equate, *inability* (to provide certain goods) with *violation*. The practical upshot of this could be to "justify" certain violations of personal rights on the grounds of present inability. We are all too familiar with this type of thing. Often enough it masquerades under the title of national security.

In conclusion, then, I believe it fair to say that the Charter aims to propose the basic justice ingredients for a public morality as this touches the family. In the remainder of this essay, I want to raise three questions about the public morality of the family: 1. What is the meaning of the term "public morality"? 2. What are the general principles of this morality where the family is concerned? 3. Does the Charter aid us in conflict situations?

The Meaning of Public Morality

The term "public morality" is frequently used, but unless I am mistaken, it is variously understood and this increases the conceptual fuzziness that surrounds the notion. Let me say first what the term does not mean, then what I believe it does mean.

Public morality in this context does not refer to the morality of public servants, interesting and important as this is. Nor does it have reference to the participation of the public on advisory groups or national policymaking commissions. That is purely formal in character. Finally, the term does not denote existing law or public policy. Such law or policy is drafted in a highly pragmatic and utilitarian process sensitive to past favors, constituency interests, and personal ambition. It has been said that there are two things we ought never see in the making: sausages and public policy.

If the notion of public morality cannot be narrowed to the three meanings noted above, then what is it? I suggest the following: Large institutions, especially the state and federal governments, are increasingly determining the social, political and economic conditions where human needs are met or not, or can be met. This is true of education, housing, health care, domestic and international security, environment, etc. The state and federal governments have many legitimate interests: reduction of welfare roles, control of illegitimacy, balancing the budget, environment, access to housing and education, defense, population equilibrium, adequate health care, to name but a few. The danger is that these legitimate interests can be pursued in a way that is one-eyed, that ends up harming individuals or families. The population policies of India during the 1960's and 70's are an example of this. Ashish Bose, India's leading demographer, has noted that India made a grave mistake when it accepted Western advice about introducing birth-control technology but failed to put enough effort into education and cultural change.[6] Closer to home, many believe things were in serious imbalance during the tenure of Caspar Weinberger at Defense.

I suggest that public morality should be understood as the balanced and harmonious pursuit of these legitimate interests, "balanced and harmonious" meaning in a way that respects the basic needs and rights of individuals and of families. This understanding of public morality is very close to what Bishop Joseph Sullivan refers to as the "rise of the moral factor in public life."[7] That a "balanced and harmonious" pursuit is not easy is obvious when one scans the periodic reports of Amnesty International. Even the Western democracies are knee-deep in the value perspectives of the culture in which they reside. They will reflect such perspectives in their policies and this will clearly affect public morality, a point powerfully made by John Paul II in *Sollicitudo rei socialis*. One need not be a Cassandra to note the pervasive influence of technology, efficiency and comfort in our thought-patterns and cultural leanings. Obviously, such perspectives can distort. They can create imbalance and disharmony in the pursuit of otherwise legitimate interests. When that happens, it is clear who will get hurt: the poor, the dependent (elderly, retarded), the marginalized, to name the most obvious .

The Principles of Public Morality

All of the rights mentioned by the Holy See's Charter can fit fairly comfortably under four general titles as follows:

1. *Respect for autonomy* (Nos. 1, 2, 3, 5, 7)

2. *Provision of goods* (Nos. 6, 9, 10, 11)

3. *Protection against harm* (Nos. 4, 6)

4. *Provision of fair access or distribution* (Nos. 9, 10. 11, 12)

Obviously, there is some overlap here because the categories themselves overlap. Thus, numbers 9-11 can fit under either 2 (provision of goods) or 4 (fair access or distribution). I advert here once again to the distinction between personal-political rights and social-economic rights. It seems clear that categories 1 (autonomy) and 3 (protection against harm) are in the personal-political category and are mostly negative in character. That is, they are satisfied by *abstention* from certain acts. Categories 2 and 4 are social-economic rights. That the family rights listed by the Charter should be organizable under four general headings is not surprising if it is remembered that *all* rights would probably fit under such general headings.

However, I do not believe that such a breakdown is trivial and without value. The general rights categories point in the direction of correlative responsibilities that can be stated as general principles. Thus:

1. The principle of autonomy.

2. The principle of beneficence.

3. The principle of non-maleficence.

4. The principle of justice.

Those familiar with the literature of bioethics will immediately recognize these as the four basic principles used to face dilemmas in that discipline.[8] I am suggesting here that they can be usefully employed as the basic principles of public morality as it touches the family. But if appeal to such principles is to be truly useful, then it must find ways of interrelating and subordinating them so they help us in conflict situations. Otherwise they will be unable to be of help where they are most needed: in constructing and criticizing policy. That brings me to my third point.

The Charter and Conflict Situations

Commenting on *Sollicitudo rei socialis,* moral theologian Leslie Griffin wrote:

> As John Paul defends such a full theory of the human person, he fails to provide a hierarchy of rights or values. The result is that John Paul's theory appears unable to deal with

the conflicts of values or conflicts of rights which arise in the concrete circumstances of human social life.[9]

Griffin's analysis of the papal encyclical is echoed by Bishop Joseph Sullivan. Sullivan notes that Catholic moral teaching has a distinct style. It is a blend of biblical and philosophical categories and John Paul II models it well as he attempts to place a religious vision at the disposal of a wider society. Sullivan then adds:

> To address the fact of poverty and injustice in our time without using the powerful style of the prophets would be an impoverishment of our best contribution to the conscience of society. Yet the prophetic categories by themselves will not allow us to engage in the complex balancing of interests and problems which a modern economy poses for anyone who would seek to move it toward greater social equity. The prophetic imperatives—do justice, care for the widows and orphans, protect the laborer, respect the alien— must be related to the complex grid of legislation and policy through which change is effected in an industrial democracy. In this task one moves beyond the resources of religious conviction and prophetic imperative to philosophical assessments of justice and empirical judgments about efficiency and effectiveness.[10]

Combining Griffin and Sullivan, I would ask: does the Charter help us "deal with the conflict of values or conflicts of rights"? Does it move us "beyond the resources of religious conviction and prophetic imperative" and aid us "in the complex balancing of interests"? I do not believe so. In this sense I believe it pertains to the category of parenetic discourse. The very same must be said of the four principles of public morality.

Let me put this a bit differently. If public morality is the harmonious and balanced pursuit of social and economic goals without infringing individual and family rights, we need, beyond a Charter, the vehicles of this harmony and balance. We need something like "mediating priority rules." This is at once the most interesting and controversial area of social ethics. It is where ethicists disagree, politicians battle, activists march, and pundits pontificate. What priorities and procedures one adopts in conflict situations says a great deal about how one is seeing the world and social reality, out of what perspective, with what hopes and moral measures.

Here I will suggest three ways that will make a mere prophetic and parenetic listing of rights or principles more useful. Much of this work has been done very well by David Hollenbach, S.J.[11] He points out that Catholic tradition possesses important principles for sorting out conflicting claims. Hollenbach points to the tripartite principle of justice (commutative, distributive, social) as insisting that both the private and public dimension of these conflicts be taken into account. The principle of subsidiarity asserts that human beings are members of several different kinds of communities. "Thus they have rightful claims to both freedom and participation." But, Hollenbach argues, "neither of these two principles . . . establishes concrete priorities for a human rights policy. This is the task of historical discernment, love and political solidarity."[12] For Hollenbach, "concrete love for persons—both as individuals and as members of society—is the only pathway to the discovery of the concrete meaning of justice and rights in a given social-political situation."[13] The particularity of discerning love will establish priorities of both goods and persons in changing social settings.

I do not want simply to repeat Hollenbach here, though some of the suggestions will root in his work.

1. *Priority of goods.* If a charter of rights is to be useful in structuring policies and programs, the underlying goods must be in some way hierarchized. Philosophers and theologians have attempted for centuries to formulate such a hierarchy. St. Thomas did this when he divided goods into exterior goods, goods of the body and spirit, etc. Such beginnings were extensively developed by Max Scheler, Nicolai Hartmann and Hans Reiner. Scheler, for instance, established a hierarchy on four levels: values of the agreeable, vital or biological values (health, vitality), spiritual values (beauty, right,

justice), and sacred values. Hartmann, and above all Reiner, developed preference principles for action when values are in conflict. These principles touch on the excellence of the value, the fundamental character of the value, its temporal urgency, its quantity, the chance of success, etc. Similar preference principles are present in traditional Catholic moral treatises under title of *ordo bonorum* and *ordo caritatis* (the determination of persons who deserve the preference). They are also implied whenever appeal is made to the notion of *ratio proportionata*.

Perhaps the term "hierarchy" is misleading. It suggests that we can line up the goods protected in the Charter's rights and give them an abstract ordinal rating that itself solves conflicts. That, I think, is unreal. In referring to infringements of rights, Langan states that they must be justified by "morally acceptable reasons, and a graduated urgency corresponding to the *varying* importance and necessity of the values that they protect."[14] Langan could and perhaps should have written "morally acceptable reasons *based on* a graduated . . ." The point I want to emphasize here is that the "graduated urgency" can root both 1) in *different* values with varying importance and necessity; 2) the *same* value with varying importance and necessity because of different circumstances. Thus, for example, life itself may be less important and necessary in some circumstances because it is not at stake or under threat.

This suggests that the "graduated urgency" mentioned by Langan is tied closely to circumstances. "Importance and necessity" can be stated apart from circumstances only in a very general, other-things-being-equal way—which is precisely what they are not in conflict situations.

This means that the "priority of goods" as a "mediating priority rule" will consist much more in formal criteria for reading situations than in material criteria. However, a discerning reading of the social situation in some places would certainly give priority to basic needs over some other social and political goods, to give but a single example.

We can see this in the concept of *ratio proportionata.* (When Langan refers to "morally acceptable reasons and a graduated urgency . . ." he is, I think, using other words for the traditional phrase *ratio proportionata.* James Walter is helpful here. He asks about the criteria for determining whether a *debita proportio* is present.[15] Walter lists six possible criteria: (1) A noncontradiction between the means and the end, or the end and further ends. (2) The means do not undermine the end. (3) The means do not cause more harm than necessary. (4) In the action as a whole, the good outweighs the evil. (5) The means are in a necessary causal relation to the end. (6) The means possess the inherent ability to effect the end. Since *debita proportio* is a broadly human assessment, and one that must be made in a wide variety of conflict situations, it should not be surprising that there are any number of ways of approaching it.

Next, Walter asks: how do we know that the criteria have been fulfilled? He lists six methods of assessment: experience, sense of profanation, trial and error, discursive reasoning, long-term consequences, the experience of harmony or guilt over our actions. Reading *debita proportio* in concrete circumstances is such a multi-faceted affair that manualist Antonius Lanza says the ultimate criterion of its correctness is the judgment of the prudent person.[16]

Here again, let me turn to Hollenbach. If love is indeed the pathway to concrete priorities, it is not difficult to understand how "love and the response of conscience to the concrete call of human dignity can precede the ability of reason to formulate moral obligation in precise moral principles."[17]

I think something similar must be said about "mediating priority rules" based on a priority of goods. Indeed, perhaps that is why the Charter remains prophetic and parenetic. Perhaps that is also why John Paul II's *Sollicitudo* does not provide a hierarchy of rights or values. Perhaps he is suggesting by omission that this cannot be done except *in situ.*

At any rate, I conclude this section by a citation from Langan.

> The work of balancing claims and interests that is the central task of political leadership is not eliminated by the notion of human rights, but the moral constraints on that process are made more clear and more emphatic. The moral evaluation of restrictions on or infringements of human rights depends on the correctness of the reasons offered in justification of the decision, on the nature and standing of the other values that are being aimed at, and on the readiness of those who decide not to satisfy a right to take other actions to preserve the rights and the well-being of persons adversely affected by their decision.[18]

If I had written that paragraph, it would have been worded a bit differently. Specifically:

> The moral evaluations of restrictions on or infringements of human rights depends on the correctness of the reasons offered in justification of the decision. These reasons root in the value behind the right being restricted, in the nature and standing of the other values that are being aimed at, etc . . .

The point I am emphasizing is that what Langan describes as "the central task of political leadership" ("the work of balancing claims and interests") looks remarkably similar to, even identical with, what an older tradition called *ratio proportionata*, as I noted.

2. *Priority of persons.* Here I shall borrow unblushingly from David Hollenbach's *Claims in Conflict.* After noting the rights listed in *Pacem in terris*, Hollenbach realistically adverts to the messy fact that in the daily pushing and shoving of economic and political life, the wants of some are met at the expense of the basic needs of others. Therefore, a truly moral rights policy must attempt to redress such imbalances. Hollenbach offers the following three moral priorities. He draws these, as noted above, from love discerning the social situation.

i) The needs of the poor take priority over the wants of the rich.

ii) The freedom of the dominated takes priority over the liberty of the powerful.

iii) The participation of marginalized groups takes priority over the preservation of an order which excludes them.[19]

Just what are such priority statements? They are not Hollenbach notes, policies. They are "normative ethical standards." Above I referred to the need of "mediating priority rules" beyond the abstract statement of rights. This is exactly the function Hollenbach envisages for his priority standards. He says of them:

> They are, however, much more proximate to the actual decisions which must be made in forming policy than are the lists of human rights found in *Pacem in terris* and the Universal Declaration. They provide a kind of guidance for the formation of policy which the lists of rights do not because they quite consciously acknowledge the fact of conflict between the claims which different persons make on the community.[20]

3. *Priority of procedure.* In *Octogesima adveniens,* Paul VI made a statement that is frequently cited.

> In the face of such widely varying situations it is difficult for us to utter a unified message and to put forward a solution which has universal validity. Such is not our ambition, nor is it our mission. It is up to the Christian communities to analyze with objectivity the situation which is proper to their own country, to shed on it the light of the Gospel's unutterable words and to draw principles of reflection, norms of judgment and directives for action from the social teaching of the Church.[21]

Paul VI's statement ("nor is it our mission") is an obvious derivative from *Gaudium et spes*. Speaking of lay people and their responsibilities the council stated:

Let lay persons not imagine that their pastors are always such experts that to every problem which arises, however complicated, they can readily give them a concrete solution, *or even that such is their mission.* Rather, enlightened by Christian wisdom and giving close attention to the teaching authority of the Church, let lay persons take on their own distinctive role.[22]

Both Paul VI and Vatican II referred to "solutions" as not belonging to their mission. Both asserted that the responsibility for solutions belongs with the communities touched by them. By "solutions" both Pope and Council mean practical application of more general standards, concrete policies and decisions. In the language used above, "solutions" would refer to the concrete decisions and policies derived from use of Hollenbach's priority standards.

I have referred to a "priority of procedure." That suggests that of several possible procedural options, one deserves the preference. What would some of the options be for the resolution of conflict situations? They could be adjudicated by an individual appointed for that purpose. They could be left to the unpredictable forces of the market. In some societies, conflicts are resolved by sheer force (armies and tanks). I am suggesting that where family rights are concerned, the preferred procedure is to involve the community insofar as possible.

This is perhaps especially true where social and economic rights are concerned. I have in mind above all the rights to food, housing, shelter, medical care, clothing, etc. Where conflicts touching these rights occur, the resolution means suffering, temporary (at least) deprivation, rationing, etc. The more the prospective sufferer participates in the decisional process, the more acceptable or at least tolerable is the outcome.

Let me take health care as an example. Several popes (e.g., *Pacem in terris*), the American bishops, and the Vatican's Charter on the Rights of the Family list health care as a right. How this is to be implemented in policy is another matter altogether. What is utterly clear is that the present health care system is not meeting the needs of many millions of uninsured or underinsured (around 37 million) persons.

There are three policy questions that face us as a nation and that will have a great deal to say about the adequacy of our health care:

i) What resources (money, energy, personnel) should go to health care in contrast to education, defense, environment, housing, commerce?

ii) Within health care, what resources (money, energy, personnel) should go to rescue (crisis) medicine in contrast to preventive medicine?

iii) In either category (rescue or prevention), who should get what when not everyone can get all?

Until we have made some organized effort to answer these questions, the right to health care will be at the mercy of market forces that have proved themselves inadequate. By "inadequate" I mean violative of the priority of goods and persons noted above.

I introduce these questions here because in the past few years there have been interesting attempts to face them, attempts that reflect the papal and conciliar conviction that such solutions belong to communities. I refer to the Community Health Decisions Movement.[23] It began in Oregon in 1983 with a series of public meetings to discuss the personal and social choices presented by the new powers of modern medicine and the escalating costs of the health care system. Thus began Oregon Health Decisions, "an organization that aims to make health care delivery more congruent with community values." As Bruce Jennings notes, science and technology have expanded medicine's power and opened a Pandora's box of complex ethical issues:

> Who should decide when the use of life-sustaining medical treatment should be foregone? On what basis should that

decision be made? What balance should be struck between preventive medicine, acute care, and chronic long-term care in what we as a nation spend on health? Does each person have a right to health care, and how can fair access to health care be guaranteed? How should scarce medical resources, like organs donated for transplantation, be rationed? Should age play a role in limiting the health care a person receives?[24]

Summing it up, Jennings notes that medicine raises "exquisitely hard questions about justice and freedom, rights and duties, benefits and harms."[25] In other words, health care—whether as a benefit, claim or right—exists in an atmosphere of profound conflict. Oregon Health Decisions is a grassroots educational attempt that aims at responsible civic participation and better informed decision-making about these conflict situations. It has inspired similar projects in at least ten different states. Oregon Health Decisions was instrumental in seeing to it that citizen opinion and community preference gave shape to important legislative decisions. This happened in 1987 when the Oregon state legislature directed limited state Medicaid funds away from costly heart and liver transplants in favor of prenatal and preventive care. It is not preposterous to see such a conclusion as congruent with the priorities listed above, and as a result of discerning love.

Health care may be unique in some ways and it would be unreal to expect all conflicted claims and rights to be dumped into a grassroots, town hall arena for an appropriate solution. The point to be underlined is that an informed and sensitive public is the best assurance that ideologies, narrowly-based interests, greedy corporations, etc., will not unduly influence practical policies that touch family rights. In this sense, one could argue that what I have called "priority of procedure" is an application of subsidiarity.

In summary, I have suggested that the rights listed and elaborated in the Charter on the Rights of the Family tend to fall into four categories (autonomy, provision of goods, protection against harm, fair access or distribution). Corresponding to these categories are four principles of public morality: principle of autonomy, of beneficence, of nonmaleficence, of justice. Just as an abstract listing of rights does not help much in devising policy in a conflicted world, so neither does a proposal of four principles of public morality. For such principles can come in conflict with one another. What is needed if the Charter on the Rights of the Family is to get nearer to the untidiness of real life is mediating priority rules that will not solve all conflicts but help us deal with them more rationally and consistently. Three were suggested: 1) priority of goods; 2) priority of persons; 3) priority of procedure.

This essay began by noting that the Charter disappeared almost as soon as it appeared. That was a judgment on its influence and impact. Perhaps that is too sweeping. To make such a judgment one would have to know its impact—or lack thereof—in developing countries. My suspicion—and it is only that—is that those who felt most urgently the need of such a Charter come from places where family rights are most frequently and grossly violated. This would be above all true of developing countries under dictatorial regimes. Perhaps, in such places, the Charter on the Rights of the Family still serves an absolutely essential prophetic and critical role. In the developed industrialized democracies of the West, the Charter is useful only insofar as we can supply the intermediate priority rules that bring it closer to policy and programs. For in these countries, the rights are most often explicitly admitted. The problem is rather practical programs and strategies to satisfy them.[26]

Notes

1. Thea Bowman, "To Be Black and Catholic," *Origins* 19 (1989).

2. Eugene Kennedy, *Tomorrow's Catholics, Yesterday's Church* (New York: Harper & Row, 1988).

3. *Charter on the Rights of the Family* (Vatican City: Vatican Polyglot Press, 1983).

4. John Langan, S.J., "Defining Human Rights: A Revision of the Liberal Tradition," in Langan and Alfred Hennelly, S.J. (eds.) *Human Rights in the Americas: The Struggle for Consensus* (Washington: Georgetown University Press, 1982).

5. Langan, 74.

6. *New York Times*, July 9, 1989, Section 4, 2.

7. Joseph Sullivan, "The Task of a Public Church," *Origins* 19 (1989) 122.

8. Cf. James Childress and Tom Beauchamp, *Principles of Biomedical Ethics* (New York: Oxford University Press, 1983).

9. Leslie Griffin, "Moral Criticism as Moral Teaching: Pope John Paul II and *Sollicitudo Rei Socialis*," in John W. Houck and Oliver F. Williams, eds., *The Recent Social Teachings of the Catholic Church*, forthcoming.

10. Joseph Sullivan, loc. cit., 123.

11. David Hollenbach, S.J., *Claims in Conflict: Retrieving and Renewing the Catholic Human Rights Tradition* (Mahwah: Paulist Press, 1979).

12. Hollenbach, 177.

13. *Ibid.*, 173.

14. Langan, 74, my emphasis.

15. James Walter, "Proportionate Reason and its Three Levels of Inquiry: Structuring the Ongoing Debate," *Louvain Studies 10* (1984) 30-40.

16. Antonius Lanza, *Theologia moralis* I (Turin: Marietti, 1949) n. 177, 208-209.

17. Hollenbach, 172.

19. Hollenbach, 204.

20. *Ibid.*, 204.

21. As in Joseph Gremillion, ed., *The Gospel of Peace and Justice* (Maryknoll: Orbis, 1976) n. 4, p. 487.

22. *The Documents of Vatican II*, ed., Walter M. Abbott, S.J., (New York: America Press, 1966) 244, emphasis added.

23. Cf. Bruce Jennings, "A Grassroots Movement in Bioethics," *Hastings Center Report* 18 (1988). Special Supplement, 3-15.

24. Jennings, 3.

25. *Loc. cit.*, 4.

26. **Charter on the Rights of the Family
Presented by the Holy See To All Persons,
Institutions and Authorities Concerned with the Mission
of the Family in Today's World**

22 October 1983

* * * *

Introduction

The "Charter of the Rights of the Family" has its origins in the request formulated by the Synod of Bishops held in Rome in 1980 on the theme: "The Role of the Christian Family in the Modern World" (cf. *Propositio* 42). His Holiness Pope John Paul II, in the Apostolic Exhortation *Familiaris Consortio* (No. 46), acceded to the Synod's request and committed the Holy See to prepare a Charter of the Rights of the Family to be presented to the quarters and authorities concerned.

It is important to understand correctly the nature and style of the Charter as it is now presented. The document is not an exposition of the dogmatic or moral theology of marriage and the family, although it reflects the Church's thinking in the matter. Nor is it a code of conduct for persons or institutions concerned with the question. The Charter is also different from a simple declaration of theoretical principles concerning the family. It aims, rather, at presenting to all our contemporaries, be they Christian or not, a formulation—as complete and ordered as possible—of the fundamental rights that are inherent in that natural and universal society which is the family.

The rights enunciated in the Charter are expressed in the conscience of the human being and in the common values of all humanity. The Christian vision is present in this Charter as the light of divine revelation which enlightens the natural reality of the family. These rights arise, in the ultimate analysis, from that law which is inscribed by the Creator in the heart of every human being. Society is called to defend these rights against all violations and to respect and promote them in the entirety of their content.

The rights that are proposed must be understood according to the specific character of a "Charter." In some cases, they recall true and proper juridically binding norms; in other cases, they express fundamental postulates and principles for legislation to be implemented and for the development of family policy. In all cases, they are a prophetic call in favour of the family institution, which must be respected and defended against all usurpation.

Almost all of these rights are already to be found in other documents of both the Church and the international community. The present Charter attempts to elaborate them further, to define them with greater clarity and to bring them together in an organic, ordered and systematic presentation. Annexed to the text are indications of "Sources and references" from which some of the formulations have been drawn.

The Charter of the Rights of the Family is now presented by the Holy See, the central and supreme organ of government of the Catholic Church. The document is enriched by a wealth of observations and insights received in response to a wide consultation of the Bishops' Conferences of the entire Church, as well as of experts in the matter from various cultures.

The Charter is addressed principally to governments. In reaffirming, for the good of society, the common awareness of the essential rights of the family, the Charter offers to all who share responsibility for the common good a model and a point of reference for the drawing up of legislation and family policy, and guidance for action programmes.

At the same time, the Holy See confidently proposes this document to the attention of intergovernmental international organizations which, in their competence and care for the defense and promotion of human rights, cannot ignore or permit violations of the fundamental rights of the family.

The Charter is of course also directed to the families themselves: it aims at reinforcing among families an awareness of the irreplaceable role and position of the family; it wishes to inspire families to unite in the defense and promotion of their rights; it encourages families to fulfil their duties in such a way that the role of the family will become more clearly appreciated and recognized in today's world.

The Charter is directed, finally, to all men and women, and especially to Christians, that they will commit themselves to do everything possible to ensure that the rights of the family are protected and that the family institution is strengthened for the good of all mankind, today and in the future.

The Holy See, in presenting this Charter, desired by the representatives of the World Episcopate, makes a special appeal to all the Church's members and institutions to bear clear witness to Christian convictions concerning the irreplaceable mission of the family, and to see that families and parents receive the necessary support and encouragement to carry out their God-given task.

Charter of the Rights of the Family

Preamble

Considering that:

A. the rights of the person, even though they are expressed as rights of the individual, have a fundamental social dimension which finds an innate and vital expression in the family;

B. the family is based on marriage, that intimate union of life in complementarity between a man and a woman which is constituted in the freely-contracted and publicly-expressed indissoluble bond of matrimony, and is open to the transmission of life;

C. marriage is the natural institution to which the mission of transmitting life is exclusively entrusted;

D. the family, a natural society, exists prior to the State or any other community, and possesses inherent rights which are inalienable;

E. the family constitutes, much more than a mere juridical, social and economic unit, a community of love and solidarity, which is uniquely suited to teach and transmit cultural, ethical, social, spiritual and religious values, essential for the development and well-being of its own members and of society;

F. the family is the place where different generations come together and help one another to grow in human wisdom and to harmonize the rights of individuals with other demands of social life;

G. the family and society, which are mutually linked by vital and organic bonds, have a complementary function in the defense and advancement of the good of every person and of humanity;

H. the experience of different cultures throughout history has shown the need for society to recognize and defend the institution of the family;

I. society, and in a particular manner the State and International Organizations, must protect the family through measures of a political, economic, social and juridical character, which aim at consolidating the unity and stability of the family so that it can exercise its specific function;

J. the rights, the fundamental needs, the well-being and the values of the family, even though they are progressively safeguarded in some cases, are often ignored and not rarely undermined by laws, institutions and socio-economic programmes;

K. many families are forced to live in situations of poverty which prevent them from carrying out their role with dignity;

L. the Catholic Church, aware that the good of the person, of society and of the Church herself passes by way of the family, has always held it part of her mission to proclaim to all the plan of God instilled in human nature concerning marriage and the family, to promote these two institutions and to defend them against all those who attack them;

M. the Synod of Bishops, celebrated in 1980, explicitly recommended that a Charter of the Rights of the Family be drawn up and circulated to all concerned;

the Holy See, having consulted the Bishops' Conferences, now presents this

Charter of the Rights of the Family

and urges all States, International Organizations, and all interested Institutions and persons to promote respect for these rights, and to secure their effective recognition and observance.

Article 1

All persons have the right to the free choice of their state of life and thus to marry and establish a family or to remain single.

a) Every man and every woman, having reached marriage age and having the necessary capacity, has the right to marry and establish a family without any discrimination whatsoever; legal restrictions to the exercise of this right, whether they be of a permanent or temporary nature, can be introduced only when they are required by grave and objective demands of the institution of marriage itself and its social and public significance; they must respect in all cases the dignity and the fundamental rights of the person.

b) Those who wish to marry and establish a family have the right to expect from society the moral, educational, social and economic conditions which will enable them to exercise their right to marry in all maturity and responsibility.

c) The institutional value of marriage should be upheld by the public authorities; the situation of non-married couples must not be placed on the same level as marriage duly contracted.

Article 2

Marriage cannot be contracted except by the free and full consent of the spouses duly expressed.

a) With due respect for the traditional role of the families in certain cultures in guiding the decision of their children, all pressure which would impede the choice of a specific person as spouse is to be avoided.

b) The future spouses have the right to their religious liberty. Therefore, to impose as a prior condition for marriage a denial of faith or a profession of faith which is contrary to conscience constitutes a violation of this right.

c) The spouses, in the natural complementarity which exists between man and woman, enjoy the same dignity and equal rights regarding the marriage.

Article 3

The spouses have the inalienable right to found a family and to decide on the spacing of births and the number of children to be born, taking into full consideration their duties towards themselves, their children already born, the family and society, in a just hierarchy of values and in accordance with the objective moral order which excludes recourse to contraception, sterilization and abortion.

a) The activities of public authorities and private organizations which attempt in any way to limit the freedom of couples in deciding about their children constitute a grave offense against human dignity and justice.

b) In international relations, economic aid for the advancement of peoples must not be conditioned on acceptance of programmes of contraception, sterilization or abortion.

c) The family has a right to assistance by society in the bearing and rearing of children. Those married couples who have a large family have a right to adequate aid and should not be subjected to discrimination.

Article 4

Human life must be respected and protected absolutely from the moment of conception.

a) Abortion is a direct violation of the fundamental right to life of the human being.

b) Respect of the dignity of the human being excludes all experimental manipulation or exploitation of the human embryo.

c) All interventions on the genetic heritage of the human person that are not aimed at correcting anomalies constitute a violation of the right to bodily integrity and contradict the good of the family.

d) Children, both before and after birth, have the right to special protection and assistance, as do their mothers during pregnancy and for a reasonable period of time after childbirth.

e) All children, whether born in or out of wedlock, enjoy the same right to social protection, with a view to their integral personal development.

f) Orphans or children who are deprived of the assistance of their parents or guardians must receive particular protection on the part of society. The State, with regard to foster-care or adoption, must provide legislation which assists suitable families to welcome into their home children who are in need of permanent or temporary care. This legislation must, at the same time, respect the natural rights of the parents.

g) Children who are handicapped have the right to find in the home and the school an environment suitable to their human development.

Article 5

Since they have conferred life on their children, parents have the original, primary and inalienable right to educate them; hence they must be acknowledged as the first and foremost educators of their children.

a) Parents have the right to educate their children in conformity with their moral and religious convictions, taking into account the cultural traditions of the family which favour the good and dignity of the child; they should also receive from society the necessary aid and assistance to perform their educational role properly.

b) Parents have the right to choose freely schools or other means necessary to educate their children in keeping with their convictions. Public authorities must ensure that public subsidies are so allocated that parents are truly free to exercise this right without incurring unjust burdens. Parents should not have to sustain, directly or indirectly, extra charges which would deny or unjustly limit the exercise of this freedom.

c) Parents have the right to ensure that their children are not compelled to attend classes which are not in agreement with their own moral and religious convictions. In particular, sex education is a basic right of the parents and must always be carried out under their close supervision, whether at home or in educational centres chosen and controlled by them.

d) The rights of parents are violated when a compulsory system of education is imposed by the State from which all religious formation is excluded.

e) The primary right of parents to educate their children must be upheld in all forms of collaboration between parents, teachers and school authorities, and particularly in forms of participation designed to give citizens a voice in the functioning of schools and in the formulation and implementation of educational policies.

f) The family has the right to expect that the means of social communication will be positive instruments for the building up of society, and will reinforce the fundamental values of the family. At the same time the family has the right to be adequately protected, especially with regard to its youngest members, from the negative effects and misuse of the mass media.

Article 6

The family has the right to exist and to progress as a family .

a) Public authorities must respect and foster the dignity, lawful independence, privacy, integrity and stability of every family.

b) Divorce attacks the very institution of marriage and of the family.

c) The extended family system, where it exists, should be held in esteem and helped to carry out better its traditional role of solidarity and mutual assistance, while at the same time respecting the rights of the nuclear family and the personal dignity of each member.

Article 7

Every family has the right to live freely its own domestic religious life under the guidance of the parents, as well as the right to profess publicly and to propagate the faith, to take part in public worship and in freely chosen programmes of religious instruction, without suffering discrimination.

Article 8

The family has the right to exercise its social and political function in the construction of society.

a) Families have the right to form associations with other families and institutions, in order to fulfil the family's role suitably and effectively, as well as to protect the rights, foster the good and represent the interests of the family.

b) On the economic, social, juridical and cultural levels, the rightful role of families and family associations must be recognized in the planning and development of programmes which touch on family life.

Article 9

Families have the right to be able to rely on an adequate family policy on the part of public authorities in the juridical, economic, social and fiscal domains, without any discrimination whatsoever.

a) Families have the right to economic conditions which assure them a standard of living appropriate to their dignity and full development. They should not be impeded from acquiring and maintaining private possessions which would favour stable family life; the laws concerning inheritance or transmission of property must respect the needs and rights of family members.

b) Families have the right to measures in the social domain which take into account their needs, especially in the event of the premature death of one or both parents, of the abandonment of one of the spouses, of accident, or sickness or invalidity, in the case of unemployment, or whenever the family has to bear extra burdens on behalf of its members for reasons of old age, physical or mental handicaps or the education of children.

c) The elderly have the right to find within their own family or, when this is not possible, in suitable institutions, an environment which will enable them to live their later years of life in serenity while pursuing those activities which are compatible with their age and which enable them to participate in social life.

d) The rights and necessities of the family, and especially the value of family unity, must be taken into consideration in penal legislation and policy, in such a way that a detainee remains in contact with his or her family and that the family is adequately sustained during the period of detention.

Article 10

Families have a right to a social and economic order in which the organization of work permits the members to live together, and does not hinder the unity, well-being, health and the stability of the family, while offering also the possibility of wholesome recreation.

a) Remuneration for work must be sufficient for establishing and maintaining a family with dignity, either through a suitable salary, called a "family wage," or through other social measures such as family allowances or the remuneration of the work in the home of one of the parents; it should be such that mothers will not be obliged to work outside the home to the detriment of family life and especially of the education of the children.

b) The work of the mother in the home must be recognized and respected because of its value for the family and for society.

Article 11

The family has the right to decent housing, fitting for family life and commensurate to the number of the members, in a physical environment that provides the basic services for the life of the family and the community.

Article 12

The families of migrants have the right to the same protection as that accorded other families.

a) The families of immigrants have the right to respect for their own culture and to receive support and assistance towards their integration into the community to which they contribute.

b) Emigrant workers have the right to see their family united as soon as possible.

c) Refugees have the right to the assistance of public authorities and International Organizations in facilitating the reunion of their families.

Where Did We Go Wrong?
The Roman Catholic Church and the Arts
Yesterday and Today

John W. O'Malley, S.J.
Weston School of Theology

During the course of Vatican Council II, many unprecedented things happened, but for our topic surely none more pertinent than the gathering that took place in the Sistine Chapel on Ascension Thursday, 7 May, 1964, 25 years ago almost to the day. In his allocution on the occasion, Pope Paul VI himself described the gathering as unique in the annals of the papacy "è la prima volta che cio si verifica,"[1] he said. The Pope celebrated Mass for a group of Italian artists and then addressed them on the subject of the relationship between them and the Catholic Church. As he pointed out, many of his predecessors had close relationships with individual artists, but none had invited them as a group to a similar encounter in which, almost as institutions of society, they expressed by their very presence to one another their close relationship.

The event and the allocution have long been forgotten by most of us. The most tangible reminder of it today is the gallery of contemporary religious art in the Vatican Museums that Paul VI created, partly as a result of this encounter, and that he opened with an equally impressive allocution on 23 May, 1973, the tenth anniversary of his pontificate.[2] In that allocution he expressed his hopes for the "flowering of a new spring of religious art in the postconciliar period."[3]

Many years have now passed since the Pope expressed those hopes, yet evidence of the "second spring," to use Newman's phrase, is not easily discerned. Some Catholics would say that noth-

95

ing has changed, others that things have changed for the worse; few indeed, as far as I know, would defend the thesis that there has been a notable change for the better. What went wrong?

I apologize for the negative wording of the question, which reflects the negative implications of my title. I hope to inject a positive note in what I have to say as I conclude. But I believe that I must begin by taking into account the common persuasion that something is ailing in the relationship between religion and the arts, and that what is incumbent upon me at the moment is to try to throw some light, from my perspective as an historian of religious culture, on the origins of the dysfunction.

As I was petitioned to do, therefore, I will address the question of the relationship between religion and the arts, but will specify that vast, vast topic by dealing with one aspect of it that is only slightly less vast and unmanageable, the relationship between the Catholic Church and the arts.

What I want to do relative to the immense scope of my topic is to review major shifts that have taken place in culture and in the Church that have affected the relationship to the arts—and by arts I mean especially architecture, painting, sculpture, and music. These shifts are, I believe, deep and important, but they are also subtle, so that they sometimes escape our perception, or at least we do not relate them very consistently to the topic at hand. I must warn you at the outset, however, to fasten your seatbelts, for we will speed through the centuries with the proverbially reckless abandon.

To locate us just a bit more firmly in time and space, however, I should like to return for a moment to Pope Paul IV's allocution to the artists in 1964. We could profitably spend all the time at our disposal in an exegesis of that remarkable address, but I will single out just a few features of it for comment. First of all, the Pope states categorically that there has from time immemorial been an intimate bond between Catholicism and the arts, a bond that he describes as a friendship. He glosses over the fact that the Christian tradition has occasionally been ambivalent about that friendship and has had to deal with strongly anti-iconic tendencies.[4] Beginning with the Hebrew Scriptures, through Tertullian and the Iconoclast heresy, and up to the Puritans of the seventeenth century, these tendencies manifested themselves in impressive ways. Nonetheless, the Pope sees the forest instead of the trees when he affirms that the history of the Church by and large is a story of a consistent and reciprocally beneficial relationship of friendship.

The Pope more than hints that this relationship is not an accident of history but is intrinsically related to the nature of the artistic and the religious (here, Christian) enterprises. They encounter each other in "spirituality," which he means to use with the fullest resonances inherent in that word. I interpret him when I say that what both religion and the arts mean to touch at their best expression is our affect, our feelings.[5]

It is true that the word "religion" means different things to different people, different things in different contexts, but it is certainly broader than either creed or code or cult. With varying degrees it includes all of them, and goes beyond, with the totality here being greater than the sum of the parts. Of the three, however, religion is most intimately related to cult, for in cult our deepest being is touched and expresses itself. Cult is not a thought or a behavior but an experience—itself an experience of the divine as well as a microcosmic expression of our other most intimate experiences of it. Like cult, art too is an expression of an inner experience, of something within that in its expression somehow transcends the individual and reaches beyond, an expression that transcends the power of words, and is thus ineffable in the literal sense of that term.[6]

That leads me to a second feature of the papal allocution. The Pope sees this relationship to cult, for he ties what he says about Catholicism and art to the Constitution on the Sacred Liturgy, *Sacrosanctum concilium*, that Vatican Council II had so recently approved. When we examine the history of Christian art, we see that in fact the vast majority of it has been executed in intimate relationship to cult. This is evident for architecture and, to a somewhat lesser degree, for music. But the fact that today most of us, especially in the United States, encounter sculpture and painting principally in museums, displaced from their original settings, somewhat inhibits our realization that it is also true for them.

We thus forget how powerfully public cult and the arts work together and how deep and connatural is their affinity. Just last year, on the occasion of the celebrations marking the millenium of Christianity in Russia, I read an account of the conversion of Prince Vladimir. The occasion for the conversion was the report of his envoys about liturgies they had experienced at the court of Byzantium. They said to him, as you possibly recall, "We knew not whether we were in heaven or on earth, for on earth there is no such splendor or beauty."[7] That statement presages the dominant role of the icon in Russian religion and religious sensibility down to our own day.[8] For the topic before us, therefore, I believe that the examination of the history of our public cult is one of our first tasks.

That brings me to a third feature of the papal allocution. Even while acknowledging the friendship between Catholicism and the arts, His Holiness simultaneously acknowledges an estrangement today. He hopes to begin to overcome the estrangement and reestablish a good relationship. He seems to be saying that the very acknowledgment that a problem exists is the first step to overcoming it. I find such an acknowledgement noteworthy in itself, and it surely clears the air for what we are about in this conference. I find it especially noteworthy, however, because the Pope does not lay the blame exclusively on the artists but recognizes that the Church itself must bear part of the responsibility.

The final feature of the allocution to which I would call your attention is in fact the character of the blame the Pope attributes to the Church. He in effect states that the Church has tried to impose inappropriate norms on the artists and judged their art with canons from a bygone era. He calls this reality a "leaden cloak" that would inhibit the artists' genius and has precluded treating them with respect as "our disciples, our friends, our partners in dialogue."[9]

I believe that Paul VI here put his finger on a critically important reason for the present situation, and it is a reason to which I shall return. I also believe, however, that it is only one factor among many, although in itself it may stand as a short-hand expression and end-result of all the others. Before we come back to it, therefore, I should like to review some other changes in religious culture that are operative today but that have their roots deep in our past.

In my opinion, the critical turning point for the issue before us was the thirteenth century, once referred to in some Catholic circles as "the greatest of the centuries." In the context in which it was used, "greatest" meant "best," thus almost precluding a review of possible shortcomings in what that century accomplished. I shall take *"greatest"* in its more obvious signification, however, to mean "biggest"—to mean most far-reaching in its implications for religion and for culture at large. Lest you misinterpret me, however, I must hasten to add that I am deeply appreciative of the truly spectacular accomplishments of that century and am ever more awed by them the more I study them. I would maintain in fact, as I hope my discussion reveals, that they were more stunning than even their most fervent eulogists seem to perceive. At the same time, I believe that, as with all major shifts in culture and religious sensibilities, we must reckon with loss as well as with gain.

Limitations of space, competence, and purpose force me to deal with only two of those accomplishments. For the first, let the university stand as a kind of condensed symbol—an absolutely crucial one for the point I want to make but also one consonant with the context in which this conference is taking place. As we all know, the university had no counterpart in the ancient world and in the earlier Middle Ages. It was a phenomenon never known before in the West, but was destined to become one of its most characteristic and influential institutions. The rapidity of its growth to maturity between the middle of the twelfth century and the beginning of the thirteenth is practically unprecedented in the history of culture.[10]

Its significance can be described in many ways. If we look at the specific intellectual problem with which especially the University of Paris was concerned during its formative years, we see, as we have so often been told, that it was the confrontation of appreciations of reality that were in possession with the body of legal codes from Roman and paleochristian antiquity and especially with the body of medical and scientific reflection from Greek antiquity. This last had for the most part not been known before and had never been systematically examined. The content of these bodies of learning account for the rapid development of the four so-called "faculties" of the University—the Faculty of Arts (or, better, of Science), the Faculty of Medicine, the Faculty of Law, and the Faculty of Theology, divisions of learning that persist in only slightly-diversified forms in our universities today.

The Faculty of Theology calls for special comment, for two reasons. First of all, that was the Faculty that most closely pertains to the subject before us. Secondly, that Faculty was a sort of hybrid reality, for it had two foci—the Bible and the body of Greek learning that for the sake of conciseness, but with some loss of accuracy, we can term "Aristotle." In other words, it was in the Faculty of Theology that the central intellectual problem of the University in the thirteenth century was most pointedly debated. We express that problem most concretely when we say it was the confrontation of Aristotle with the Bible, more generally when we say the confrontation of reason with revelation, most generally when we say the confrontation of the products of human culture with claims of transcendency.

We have no time for an examination of the ramifications of that aspect of what the university meant. Since it has been so amply treated by scholars in the past 50 years, I want to move on to what I consider a more profound shift in what the University, especially in the Faculty of Theology, signified and one that is so big that it easily escapes our consideration.

I want to speak of a subtle but absolutely crucial shift in cultural sensibilities. I want to speak of what I would describe as a quantum leap in the ongoing movement in Western civilization from an oral culture to a literate culture. I believe that the thirteenth century was a most significant step in that direction, whose next great landmark was the invention of printing in the sixteenth century, which in turn finally led to the electronic devices of our own generation.

In recent years, anthropologists have written a great deal about the characteristics of so-called oral cultures, especially as found in more primitive societies than the West in the twelfth and thirteenth centuries. I believe, nonetheless, that much of what they say applies to that situation. I obviously have my own ideas on this subject, but I have to admit being deeply influenced by the writings of Walter Ong, especially his *Orality and Literacy*. Father Ong does not, however, apply what he says so specifically as I do on this occasion.[11]

Here is what happened, in brief, in the thirteenth century. Theology moved from the episcopal *cathedral* and the monastic chapel to the classroom. It moved from a primarily liturgical context to one that was professedly academic or even "scientific." If we say that the Bible moved from the chapel to the classroom, we must realize that this move made the Bible a very different book from what it was before. From being a book of devotion, it became a data-base— a source of information about the sacred with which to confront the "natural theology" of Aristotle.

I am very much aware that the Bible was mined as a source of information about God and the world before the thirteenth century, but one has only to read the homilies of Bernard or the homilies and even the treatises of Augustine and compare them with the *Summa theologiae* of Saint Thomas to get some idea of what I am driving at. Even Bernard, "the last of the Fathers," was heir to the rhetorical traditions that influenced the patristic tradition. Both Bernard and

Augustine "did theology," but they did it "in a different key" than the scholastics of the thirteenth and subsequent centuries.

Even though the works of Augustine and Bernard were eventually written down, they bear many of the characteristics that Ong singles out as belonging to oral culture.[12] Both Augustine and Bernard obviously assumed, for instance, in the power of the sounded rather than the written or the thought word. Although they often began with a text from Scripture, their discourse is marked by the mnemonic devices and formulas typical of oral cultures as they took off from the text. Such devises and formulas are intimately related to rhythm, and thus to music—and thereby to affect.

Moreover, the style of these works was additive rather than subordinate, aggregative rather than analytic, redundant and evocative rather than characterized by precise definition of terms and the progression of logical argument. It was poetical and rhetorical, as befitted the often liturgical or quasi-liturgical setting in which it was first developed. As such, once again, it touched the affect as much as the mind. The authors believed, moreover, that their style was consonant with the nature of the Scriptures they were expounding, for it was their restless *hearts,* as much as their minds, that found rest in the sacred text.

Nothing was more characteristic of the schoolmen or scholastics, that is, of the university professors of the thirteenth century, than their penchant for definition of terms, determination of precise conclusions, disputateous or dialectical progression of argument. They thus relentlessly quested, (with their *quaestiones*) for greater clarity than rested in serene contemplation. For fulfillment, this penchant presupposes a culture characterized by what Ong calls literacy, by analytic rather than rhetorical examination of texts. While recognizing the uses of the so-called allegorical or applied or "poetic" senses of Scripture, for instance, the scholastics in principal opted for the literal, which was surely more in keeping with their own "scientific" enterprise. They were concerned with analysis that would lead to precise conclusions of doctrine.

With them, in fact, the word "doctrine" underwent an important redefinition. It came to mean more exclusively an intellectual ascent to abstract propositions, especially in the form of conclusions to dialectical argumentation. They thus undercut the affective dimension typical of the "rhetorical theology" of the Fathers. Bernard and Thomas may teach the same abstract idea of grace, but they do so, as I said, in a different key. Better put, the tune (that is, the doctrine) may be the same, but the music is different, or perhaps even lacking in the second case, replaced by cacophony.

For the rhetorical or patristic tradition, theology was by virtue of its affective dimension inseparable from what we call "spirituality." The scholastic enterprise marked the first and decisive parting of the ways between the two, a parting of the ways that subsequent centuries have tried in vain to overcome. The scholastics, surely building on some tendencies already present from earlier centuries, gave us our definitions of "doctrine" and "the teaching of the Church" as we commonly understand them today.

This is what I mean when I say that the scholastics sent us on a path that I would describe as the "doctrinalization" of Christianity. Included in that path was a new and implicit "rage for orthodoxy" that only gradually manifested itself. Later monuments to that doctrinalization would be the zeal for catechesis that burst forth in the sixteenth century and that showed itself so powerful in the extensive system of primary and secondary schools that marked the Church in the United States from the late nineteenth through most of the twentieth century. What is included here is a subtle shift in religious values and sensitivities, as proof marginalizes affect, as analysis substitutes for poetry, as univocal definition of terms replaces poetic ambiguity, as mind takes precedence over heart, as the very nature of language changes from one charged with affective and aesthetic resonances to one that is typified by analysis, critical argument, and, in some instances, pat answers to mystery.

I believe that these new appreciations gradually permeated every aspect of our consciousness and gradually led us, in practice if not in theory, to assign secondary importance to affect in religion and, consequently, to the arts. I have heard many times the stricture leveled at certain liturgies, "Oh, the people come only to hear the good music." I doubt the accuracy of that criticism, for, especially today, people can hear better music elsewhere. These people, I would maintain, have a better sense of what is involved in true liturgy than their critics. A distinguished scholar recently observed, for instance, that historians of liturgy have consistently neglected the study of the non-verbal elements in that story, although those elements are, he insists, "possibly the most important part of liturgy."[13] By way of example, he recalled how different is the *ethos* of a Mass by Palestrina from one by Mozart. The relentless "rubricism" of modern Roman Catholicism, including its resurgence in the past ten years, is a practical symptom of the misplaced emphasis that has touched every one of us on a Sunday morning.

Let me now move to the second development in the thirteenth century that had a lasting and ever-growing impact. The mendicant orders, like the Dominicans and Franciscans, responded to a new interest in preaching that marked that century, and it is no accident that the official name the disciples of St. Dominic chose for themselves was the Order of Preachers. Given the intimate relationship these orders had with the nascent universities, we should expect their sermons to be marked by the new understanding of doctrine that was, somewhat unwittingly, being propounded in those institutions. To a great extent they were, but even more characteristic of them was their moralizing. One of the reasons these preachers turned to this alternative was perhaps the highly-intellectualized "doctrine" they learned in their studies, a style of doctrine not particularly consonant with the conversion of heart that the friars, especially the Franciscans, saw as central to their religious purposes.

In any case, the preaching of the friars is commonly characterized as "penitential," that is, having conversion from vice to virtue as its primary purpose. It dealt, therefore, with the emotions, especially fear, but encased them in a moralistic framework. In my opinion, the most influential words ever uttered about preaching, if we exclude the New Testament itself, occur in the short ninth chapter of the correlatively short *Rule of St. Francis.* The Saint tells his friars that in their preaching they are to deal with "vice and virtue, punishment and glory."[14]

From the records that have come down to us, we have incontrovertible evidence of the seriousness with which Franciscan preachers took up this charge and the degree that they incorporated it into their sermons. It much influenced the Dominicans as the years moved on, and the other orders of mendicant friars as well. The famous decree on preaching of the Council of Trent paraphrases it without revealing the source,[15] and the Rule thus became the official canon for Catholic preaching from that date forward, quoted again and again by theorists in their books on the "art of preaching" or "ecclesiastical rhetorics," as they came to be called. As I have been able to show elsewhere, alternatives to this moralistic emphasis were proposed and practiced, but they could never displace the centrality of that tradition.[16]

Along with the "doctrinalization" of Christianity, therefore, the thirteenth century gave impulse to a new "moralization" of Christianity, to a stronger impulse to criticize the *mores* of individuals and of society at large in all its aspects. An important manifestation of this impulse, particularly pertinent to our topic, is the decree of the Council of Trent on sacred images.[17] First of all, the "doctrinalizing" or didactic impulse surfaces in the statement that such images are meant as instruction "in the articles of faith." It then goes on to condemn "all lasciviousness," and orders the bishops to eliminate from them anything that may appear "disorderly and unbecoming."

The decree, although surely intended to deal with real abuses, also delivered into the hands of churchmen a potential censoriousness relative to art that had never before been so effectively codified. It also suggests the possibility of more explicit use of art as propaganda, of art as a service to ideology rather than a spontaneous expression of personal or communal faith and feeling. It is one of the remote origins, I believe, of the "leaden cloak" to which Paul VI referred in his allocution of 1964. Implicit and explicit norms about what constituted the new genre that came to be known as "sacred art" or "religious art" began to be formulated by persons with little or no aesthetic appreciation, by persons of limited refinement in the arts. Doctrinal content and moral suitability assumed a new stature that in lesser spirits could easily degenerate into pompous judgmentalism. The best known and most obvious monuments to this attitude fell outside the arts but promoted the mindset. I refer to the various Indexes of Prohibited Books and the founding of the Inquisition or Holy Office, both of which were instituted in the sixteenth century for the first time and were in full swing by the end of the century.

Certain bishops after Trent took seriously the decree concerning images, as we know from the cases of Saint Charles Borromeo, archbishop of Milan, and of Gabriel Paleotti, archbishop of Bologna.[18] However, its wording was vague enough, the means of communication were rudimentary enough, society was localized enough, and education was unorganized enough for it not to make as much of an impression as we might at first think. It did, nonetheless, provide the warrant for developments that by the nineteenth century could take sure and widespread form.

Had it or its equivalent been applied in the early sixteenth century, it surely would have inhibited, for instance, the greatest single masterpieces in the Vatican. I refer to Michelangelo's frescoes on the ceiling of the Sistine Chapel and his "Last Judgment" painted there on the altar wall—with their blatant frontal nudity, female and male. A few decades after the "Last Judgment" was completed, however, certain figures in that fresco were overpainted with appropriate draperies, as is well known and justly deplored.

While we have been examining the censoriousness of the Tridentine decree, we must also reckon with the fact that it embodied an implicit recognition of a relationship between religion and art and an implicit condemnation of the iconoclastic tendencies of some

Protestant reformers.[19] In that sense, it was a reaffirmation of the central tradition in this regard and was understood as such. Moreover, for the reasons I have enumerated, there were many pockets in society where, for the most part, the new judgmentalism took a long, long time to penetrate, even after the Council. The Vatican was surely one of these pockets, but there were many others. In Rome in the seventeenth century, cardinals, prelates, and superiors of religious orders enthusiastically commissioned paintings by Caravaggio, although the sensuality of some of his paintings was almost palpable. It was well known, moreover, that he sometimes used prostitutes as models, even for paintings of the Virgin Mary, and he was himself known for his sexual promiscuity.

If the Jesuits were affected by the censorious aspect of the Tridentine decree, they interpreted it in an intelligent and benign sense, as their great churches in Rome especially testify. Whatever the "Catholic Reform" the Jesuits espoused signified, it surely did not signal a nostalgic and sentimental return to artistic forms of bygone eras—they built baroque churches, not gothic ones, and employed the most distinguished artists of their day. In their mission to the Guarani of Paraguay, their imaginative fostering of the musical talents of the Indians and their employment of them inside and outside the liturgy is legendary. Their schools around the world were famous not only for the remarkable theater they produced, but in some instances also for their cultivation of dance, specifically the ballet.[20] At the *Collège Louis le Grand* in Paris, for instance, the king and members of his court often came to see the ballet performances of the students. It must be admitted, however, that the ventures of the Jesuits into fields like theater and dance often had a more pronounced didactic and propagandistic aspect to them than would have been verified in earlier times, another hint as to the course so-called religious art would increasingly follow.

Some historians see even the Council of Trent effecting another, perhaps even deeper, change in Catholic religious practice that is pertinent for our topic. According to them, the medieval Church, for all its faults, operated through a network of natural "kinships" that meant that religion was woven into the fabric of family, neighbor-hood, and voluntary associations with a spontaneity that we find difficult to comprehend and recapture. They found and expressed their devotion in guilds, confraternities, third orders, manor chapels, and local shrines. What catechesis lacked in systematic or-ganization, it compensated for by the intimacy of the instruction given by parents and godparents.[21]

The emphasis that the Council of Trent placed on the parish and its pastor as the normative location for religious practice symbol-ized a momentous change in the offing and began to undercut the medieval network of more spontaneous and "natural" relation-ships. The great wave of organized catechesis and confessional schools that followed in the wake of the Council contributed to the same end. The creation of these "public institutions" gradually un-dercut familial responsibilities and formalized religious practice to a degree hitherto unknown. With the erection of seminaries, future pastors got separated from the popular culture into which they had been born. When they returned to it, they returned as aliens. As bishops took ever-greater responsibility for the appointment of pas-tors, the people began to lose their role in designating one of their own as their religious leader. The intensely local character of medieval religion was replaced by something more distant, more impersonal, even more bureaucratic. The invention of printing and the generally-increased facility of travel and communication during the period in question promoted the change to a degree that would have been impossible earlier.

Although a certain nostalgic romanticism about the Middle Ages can sometimes be detected in this analysis, as well as a perhaps too indulgent view of the problems rampant in the late-medieval Church, these critics have put their finger on something of immense importance concerning the way the Church has changed in the past 400 years. The institutional aspects of the Church emerged more forcefully, with a concomitant lessening of engagement on the part of both high and low in society. Religious feeling became channeled into predetermined molds and was made to conform to norms established from above and beyond.

The cultural shifts within the Church that I have been describing remained dissipated and sometimes almost latent until the nineteenth century, which is when they began to appropriate their contemporary and aggressive forms. The aftermath of the French Revolution brought with it a great reaction to all that the Revolution seemed to symbolize. It was the age of restorations—restorations to presumably happier times when proper order prevailed. Nowhere was this quest for order and its concomitant distrust of modernity more operative than in the Church, which had suffered such trauma for its made-in-heaven marriage with the *ancien régime*. The many pronouncements of Pope Pius IX, especially his "Syllabus of Errors," are emblematic of this new psychological reality. In a new key the Church was now the watchdog of doctrine, the censor of morals, the set-apart and set-above judge of society and culture, which was now characterized by aberrations too numerous to mention.

A sadly amusing illustration that shows that this attitude did not die with the nineteenth century or even with Vatican II is the single sentence that the editors of the English-language edition of the *Osservatore Romano* highlighted from Pope Paul's allocution about contemporary art, 6 May, 1973. Although the sentence was quite untypical of the allocution as a whole, the editors placed it in bold print in the margin of the paper's reprint of the full text. The sentence reads, as if it were a summary of the papal message: ". . . modern art is not solely the product of madness, passion and arbitrary abstraction."[22]

I am not a psychologist, but I would understand that the harsh judmentalism that this editorial decision betrays generally indicates a personality out of touch with its own feelings or affect, a dysfunction that deeply influences one's relationship with the other, whoever that other may be. If this interpretation has any weight, it surely says something about the relationship of the Church with art, which is so deeply related itself to affect and feeling.

In any case, as part of the Church's being set-apart and set-above society, a new interpretation was gradually advanced towards the end of the nineteenth century for the Tridentine decree on seminaries.[23] The decree itself looked to "the sons of the poor" and to the education of the lower clergy, and was never intended to apply universally to all candidates for the priesthood, many of whom had much better educational opportunities available to them. Bit by bit, however, the decree was extended to make seminary training a precondition for ordination to the priesthood, and today the term "seminary" is officially being applied even to the schools run by religious orders for their own members.[24] Surely, until quite recently, members of aristocratic families from whom the higher clergy was generally drawn never dreamed that their sons should receive their education in such a lowly institution as a seminary.

I mention this development for it relates to the question of patronage, an indispensable consideration for our topic. While it is true that we cannot point to any single patron for the great Romanesque and Gothic churches of the Middle Ages, by the fifteenth century patronage emerged in the Italian Renaissance as inseparably united with the flourishing of all the arts. That patronage was in the hands of a cultural elite, who had the financial means, to be sure, to undertake this function, but also had the leisure to cultivate taste for the arts and to see in them an enhancement and expression of their most deeply held values. In this role they had a freedom to express their taste, whether it coincided with convention or ran counter to it. They did not have to win the approval of a committee. Their mistakes would be buried with them, but their prophetic eccentricities would win them the admiration of succeeding generations. I shudder to think what would have been the fate of the Sistine Ceiling had Michelangelo been responsible to anybody except the public-opinion-be-damned Pope Julius II.

In any case, at least since the fifteenth century the patronage of most art related to cult and religion has been in the hands of churchmen. As all churchmen began not only to be trained in seminaries, but seminaries in the restorationist style of the nineteenth century—set apart from general culture and usually in opposition to it—there had to be negative repercussions on the relationship between religion and the arts, including folk art.

Just two years after the *Seminario Romano,* the seminary for the diocese of Rome, was founded in 1564 and put under the supervision of the Jesuits, no less a person than Giovanni Pierluigi Palestrina was hired as *Maestro di Capella,* despite the Jesuits' caution about training in chant and liturgical music for their own members.[25] I know of no institution for the training of the Catholic clergy today where a musician (or even musicologist) or an art connoisseur (or even art historian) holds the most prestigious chair. In fact, I know of only a few Catholic seminaries where the arts figure into the program at all, despite the renewed emphasis on liturgy as central to Catholic devotion promoted by Vatican II.[26] To a lesser degree, the same generalization could be made for most other Catholic institutions of higher learning in the United States and elsewhere. Religion has come to mean doctrine and morals, though we now make some concession for "spirituality" as long as it is done out of printed books and remains a classroom exercise.

What I have been trying to show up to this point has been that the Church's journey to the sentimental land of *kitsch* has been long and tortuous, and it does not admit of facile reversal of course. It has as its milestones complex shifts in religious values and sensibilities that are deep within our consciousness, so deep that they almost defy the telling. My own telling is surely debatable in many ways; it is, for one thing, desperately lopsided.

I have spoken, that is, as if these shifts were due almost exclusively to conscious or semi-conscious decisions within the Church, whereas we know that the Church is itself just one symbiotic element in the larger reality of culture and civilization at large. Although the Church in its social dimension sometimes resists that larger reality, it more generally reflects it and is interpenetrated by it.

Let me give just one illustration of what I mean. Why did Florence become in the fifteenth century the matrix for perhaps the most splendid flowering of painting, sculpture, and architecture the world has ever seen? We can never arrive, of course, at any satisfactory answer to the question, and perhaps the best we can do is provide a grocery list of factors that were operative, realizing that even their sum falls far short of explaining that brilliant burst of human genius. The rise of Florence as a commercial and banking center provided the resources for patronage, for instance, but in our own age of unprecedented personal wealth we seem to await in vain a similar flowering.

Somehow it comes down to a question of values, but then we must ask: "Whence the values?" If we look at Florence in the fifteenth century, we see that it was, despite its commercial success, still a society of artisans. From the artisans came the artists, to make a distinction that was hardly known to the fifteenth century. The artisans were masters of their crafts and proud of them. As is generally the case, the better among them became intent not only in producing the useful, the *utile*, but also the beautiful, the *pulchrum*. Surrounded as they were with examples of the beautiful from antiquity and spurred to emulation by their many competitors, the beautiful assumed a centrality in the lives of both artisans and patrons that is a precondition for what happened in Florence. In a more industrialized and even technological society, in an even more intensely commercial society, that precondition erodes.

When we add to the industrial and technological center of interest of contemporary society the impact upon us of the modern media of communication, the telling becomes even more complicated. With television, for instance, we are almost force-fed from our earliest days with glitz and what is known as entertainment, and this fills the space formerly occupied, at least in the lives of the best of the leisured classes, by the *pulchrum*; the artisan class has almost disappeared. The media, moreover, cut across all classes of society, all professions, all ages. Even as an ideal the cultivation of good taste has much to overcome.

I will not even try to deal with the immense problem of the evolving alienation from the Church of the cultural and intellectual elite in the West, of which we begin to have clear indications very early in the periods we have been considering and which has now become the status quo. While the Church was rejecting the "modern world," the "modern world" was rejecting the Church—in an interplay in which it is almost impossible judiciously to assign praise and blame. I do believe, however, that some of the factors on the side of the Church upon which I have been elaborating contributed mightily to the estrangement, to the break-up of the friendship that Pope Paul VI described specifically as the traditional and connatural relationship between the Church and the arts.

I will at this point conclude my jeremiad and descend from my vast generalities to the Jesuit Institute of Boston College that we are inaugurating. I will change roles from censor of the censorious to consoler of those who, by this point in my discourse, must badly need consolation. This consolation rests, however, on the modesty implicit in the tradition of Christian spirituality that tells us that no more is expected of us than to accept with serenity what we cannot change and ask for the courage to change what we can. We leave the rest to a power greater than ourselves. John the Baptist was a voice crying in the wilderness, but eventually he was heard and had impact. For the issue before us, the Institute may feel that it is a similarly lonely voice, but maybe its example will lead others to join it.

The Institute will form part of Boston College. From what I have said, it must seem that I consider a university as a rather strange ally in the effort to overcome the estrangement between the Church and the arts, and indeed I do. Since they were first founded in the thirteenth century, universities do not have a history as a seedbed of creativity in the arts. To some extent they have been, if not enemies of the arts, at least rivals and espousers of a style of culture that is somewhat of an antithesis to them.

Despite this history, academic culture and artistic culture both stand for visions that rise above convention, and in that feature they find a kinship, uneasy though it may be. Especially in recent decades, universities have on occasion taken poets and successful writers of fiction under their wings and provided places for them on the faculty—and it is in literature that the academy and artistic creativity most naturally intersect. It is, of course, in today's undergraduate colleges that future writers, for the most part, finish their remote preparation for their craft. Even more, some universities have departments that not only study art but also provide training and studios for those who aspire to becoming sculptors or painters, and there are, of course, the schools of architecture and music.

In other words, despite the gap that has in many ways held the academic world apart from the arts, the universities have become one of the major institutions to which we look for vision beyond the moment and even for the fostering of higher culture in general. We look to them to resist cheap solutions and orthodoxy on demand, no matter from whom the demands come and no matter whether they relate to religion or to culture in general.

Moreover, as I have implied, universities have to some extent assumed functions formerly held in an apprenticeship system by the master artist and assumed some of the functions of the patron. They strive not only to analyze what has happened, their more traditional role, but now also to promote creativity for the future. The undergraduate college retains the powerful role it developed for fashioning taste, especially as that college evolved in the nineteenth century from the *lycée, Gymnasium,* or *collège* that were the Jesuits schools in the United States. I see these newer roles as consonant with the Jesuit Institute.

In a university like Boston College that prides itself on being in the Catholic and Jesuit tradition, these roles should correlate with theology and the practice of religion. "Atmosphere" is a vague word that denotes a vague reality, but a reality nonetheless. I believe that Jesuit schools by the very fact of their existence, stand for the compatibility of Christianity and culture, but we must reeducate ourselves to understand Christianity as something more than "doctrine" and "morals," and culture as something more than books and analysis. More basic still, the whole university must be prophetic enough in relationship even to similar institutions in today's world to stand for something more than "getting ahead" in business and technology.

Experience of the transcendent and expression of it, however inadequate and however defined, is where religion and the arts meet. Their privileged meeting place has traditionally been public cult. The university is, of course, not a cathedral, and we must resist current efforts to turn it into one. But in a Catholic university we should expect cult to be practiced as well as appropriately studied. The cult should, therefore, foster the artistic component that is proper to it, whether on the so-called folk level or another. The study should strive to overcome our academic prejudice in favor of texts and ideas and try to devise means for appreciating the non-verbal and non-cerebral elements that so intrinsically constitute it. The aesthetic dimension to theology in general is now being increasingly recognized and needs to be encouraged.[27]

These are big orders for a little Institute. If the Institute frames those orders in the modesty I earlier advocated, if it proceeds one day at a time, however, it will not feel utterly overwhelmed, and it can begin to accomplish something. The interdisciplinary implications of the orders perhaps suggest that an "institute" may be the instrument suitable for such beginnings. In any case, the Institute can never say that there is not a problem to be addressed in the relationship between the Church and the arts, and it can rest certain that there are people out there who will be reassured and gratified even by the effort.

Notes

1. The allocution is reprinted in *Acta Apostolicae Sedis* 56 (1964) 438-44; henceforth, *AAS*. The quotation is from p. 438. See the commentary in *America* 110 (May 23, 1964) 704. See also Gaston Savorin, "Echo du colloque: 'Paul VI et les arts,'" *La Maison-Dieu* 173 (1988) 143-52.

2. See *AAS*, 65 (1973) 391-95. Attention might also be called to Paul VI's allocution to representatives of the "media of communication" (radio, film, and television) on 6 May, 1967, *AAS* 59 (1967) 505-9.

3. *AAS* 65 (1973) 394, ". . . la fioritura di una primavera nuova dell'Arte religiosa postconciliare."

4. On these tendencies, see, e.g., Samuel Laeuchli, *Religion and Art in Conflict: Introduction to a Cross-Disciplinary Task* (Philadelphia: Fortress Press, 1980), esp. 57-86.

5. See, e.g., Wassily Kandinsky, "Concerning the Spiritual in Art" in *Art, Creativity, and the Sacred: An Anthology in Religion and Art*, ed. Diane Apostolos-Cappadona (New York: Crossroad, 1984), 3-7, and Paul Tillich, "Art and Ultimate Reality," *ibid.*, 219-35.

6. See e.g., Karl Rahner, "Theology and the Arts," *Thought*, 57 (1982) 17-29.

7. As reported by Serge Schmemann in an article entitled "Gorbachev and Church: Soviet Leader's New Tolerance Recognizes that 1000 Year Grip Is Not Easily Broken," *The New York Times* (16 June, 1988) A12.

8. See, e.g., Richard F. Gustafson, *Leo Tolstoi, Resident and Stranger: A Study in Fiction and Theology* (Princeton: Princeton University Press, 1986). I am indebted to Rev. Philip C. Rule, S.J., The College of the Holy Cross, for this reference.

9. *AAS* (1964) 441, "una cappa di piombo"; "Non vi abbiamo avuti allievi, amici, conversatori: perciò voi non ci avete conosciuti."

10. See my essay, with bibliography, "The Jesuit Educational Enterprise in Historical Perspective," in *Jesuit Education: The Challenge of the 1980's and Beyond*, ed. Rolando E. Bonaches (Pittsburgh: Duquesne University Press, 1989) 10-25.

11. *Orality and Literacy: The Technologizing of the Word* (London and New York: Methuen, 1982). See also his *The Presence of the Word: Some Prolegomena for Cultural and Religious History* (New Haven and London: Yale University Press, 1967), and *Interfaces of the Word: Studies in the Evolution of Consciousness and Culture* (Ithaca and London: Cornell University Press, 1977).

12. See *Orality and Literacy*, 31-77.

13. Niels Krogh Rasmussen, "Liturgy and the Liturgical Arts," in *Catholicism in Early Modern History: A Guide to Research*, ed. John W. O' Malley (St. Louis: Center for Reformation Research, 1988) 285.

14. See "The Rule of 1223," in *St. Francis of Assisi, Writings and Early Biographies: English Omnibus of the Sources for the Life of St. Francis*, ed. Marion A. Habig, 3rd rev. ed. (Chicago: Franciscan Herald Press [1977]) 63. See also my "Form, Content, and Influence of Works about Preaching before Trent: The Franciscan Contribution," in *I Frati Minori tra '400 e '500: Atti del XII convegno internazionale* (Assisi: Edizioni Scientifiche Italiane, 1985) 27-50.

15. Fifth Session, "Decree concerning Reform," chapter 2. See the English translation, *The Canons and Decrees of the Council of Trent*, trans. H. J. Schroeder (Rockford, IL: Tan Books and Publishers, 1978) 26.

16. See, e.g., my *Praise and Blame in Renaissance Rome: Rhetoric, Doctrine, and Reform in the Sacred Orators of the Papal Court, ca.1450-1520* (Durham: Duke University Press, 1979).

17. Twenty-fifth Session, "On the Invocation, Veneration, and Relics of Saints, and on Sacred Images," in *Canons and Decrees* 216-217.

18. On Borromeo, see, e.g., E. Cecilia Volker, "Borromeo's Influence on Sacred Art and Architecture," in *San Carlo Borromeo: Catholic Reform and Ecclesiastical Politics in the Second Half of the Sixteenth Century,* ed. John M. Headley (Washington: University Press of America, 1988) 172-87. On Paleotti, see Giuiseppe Olmi and Paolo Prodi, "Art, Science, and Nature in Bologna Circa 1600," in *The Age of Correggio and the Carracci: Emilian Painting of the Sixteenth and Seventeenth Centuries* (Washington, New York, and Bologna: National Gallery of Art, The Metropolitan Museum of Art, Pinacoteca Nazionale, 1986) 213-35.

19. See, e.g., Carl C. Christensen, "Reformation and Art," in *Reformation Europe: A Guide to Research,* ed. Steven Ozment (St. Louis: Center for Reformation Research, 1982) 249-70.

20. On Jesuit theater, see, e.g., Jean-Marie Valentin, *Le théâtre des jésuites dans les pays de langue allemande,* 3 vols. (Bern, Frankfurt, Las Vegas: P. Lang, 1978). On ballet, see Raymond, Lebegue, "Les ballets des jésuites," *Revue des cours et conferences 37* (1936) 127-39, 209-22, 321-30. Further references can be found in László Polgár, *Bibliographie sur l'histoire de la Compagnie de Jésus 1901-80,* 3 vols. to date (Rome: Institutum Historicum S. I., (1981-).

21. John Bossy is the principal exponent of this viewpoint. See, e.g., his "The Counter Reformation and the Peoples of Catholic Europe," *Past and Present,* no. 47 (May, 1970) 51-70, and now his *Christianity in the West 1400-1700* (Oxford and New York: Oxford University Press, 1985).

22. *Osservatore Romano* [English language edition], (12 July, 1973) 7.

23. Twenty-third Session, "Decree concerning Reform," chapter 18, in *Canons and Decrees* 175-79.

24. I trace this development in my "Houses of Study of Religious Orders and Congregations: A Historical Sketch," in *Reason for the Hope: A Study of the Futures of Roman Catholic Theologates,* ed. Katarina Schuth (Wilmington: Michael Glazier, 1989) 29 - 45. See also my "Diocesan and Religious Models of Formation: Historical Perspectives" in *Priests: Identity and Mission,* ed. Robert Wister (Wilmington: Michael Glazier, 1990) 54-70.

25. See Ricardo García Villoslada, "Algunos dócumentos sobre la musica en el antiguo seminario romano," *Archivum Historicum Societatis Jesu 31* (1962) 107-38.

26. For some suggestions as to how this might be done, see John W. Cook, "The Arts in Theological Education for the Church," *Theological Education* 25 (1988) 22-434, and Wilson Yates, *The Arts in Theological Education: New Possibilities for Integration* (Atlanta: Scholars Press, 1987). See also the new periodical, *Arts: The Arts in Religious and Theological Studies, 1988—* .

27. See, e.g., Thomas Franklin O'Meara, "The Aesthetic Dimension in Theology," in *Art, Creativity, and the Sacred* 219-35.

On Not Running the Territorial Metaphor into the Ground: Toward a New Paradigm for Interdisciplinary Studies

Anne E. Patrick, SNJM
Carleton College

"Where did we go wrong?" John O'Malley asks a crucial question in the preceding chapter on interrelating religion and the arts. Most appropriately, he concentrates on where the Catholic Church has gone wrong, on how in modern times it has failed to live up to a rich tradition of fostering the arts. But surely we may expand the "we" in this question, "Where did we go wrong?," and ask it not only of the religious culture of Catholicism but also of some other actors on the Western stage. The question can profitably be addressed, for example, to the literary culture of Matthew Arnold and later critics and theorists of literature, who have lurched from extravagant claims for the salvific power of texts to theories about the impossibility of interpreting texts, much less being saved by them. Likewise it can be asked of the philosophical culture of Immanuel Kant and the moralists influenced by his theorizing, who have tended to divorce thought from feeling, and to focus on action abstracted from contextual concerns of affectivity and character. Indeed, it can and should be put to the entire androcentric culture of Western civilization as we have known it since the dawn, or more properly, the creation of patriarchy.[1] For various reasons, I shall select the post-Arnoldian literary culture for attention here, using this case as a point of entry into broader considerations about how we think about disciplines and the relations among them. Rather than concentrating entirely on the discordant records of where we have gone wrong, however, I shall complement my critique of literary and academic cultures with some constructive ideas on the next question, namely, "How can we do better?" Both the critical and constructive things I say will draw on some insights from St. Ignatius, whose charism still has much to offer a university at the close of this second millennium of Christian history.

I. The Case of Anglo-American Literary Culture

About a decade ago there appeared two jeremiads, one concerning literature and the other literary criticism, which brought to attention problems in Anglo-American literary culture where religion and ethics are concerned. In a provocative polemic, *On Moral Fiction*, the late novelist John Gardner berated most of his contemporaries for succumbing to moral relativism and wasting time on trivialities.[2] And in an impressive scholarly volume, *The Failure of Criticism*, Eugene Goodheart lamented the loss of an authoritative humanist criticism.[3] Although neither author achieved a fully satisfactory diagnosis, Gardner and Goodheart were both struggling to describe a network of problems afflicting the literary-cultural scene. Both recognized that "pluralism" or "plurality" is a condition of contemporary life, and both were concerned with the loss of authority that this condition entails.[4] How can differences of opinion about values be resolved, how can value conflicts be mediated in a society committed to tolerance, to accepting pluralism as a way of art and life? Such are the questions preoccupying Gardner and Goodheart in these volumes.

In these works, both writers acknowledged that there is something religious involved in the dilemma they discuss. Yet puzzlingly, although they were concerned directly with morality and religion, neither Gardner nor Goodheart drew on the resources of the disciplines traditionally concerned with moral and religious experience, namely, ethics and theology. This leads me to ask whether the reason for the limited success of these critical works may have something to do with their attempting to deal with a complex reality—one whose dimensions are moral and religious as well as literary—with chiefly critical categories, supplemented by the informal thoughts on religion and morality that happened to be part of the given writer's personal stock of ideas.

The author of *Nickel Mountain, October Light,* and other novels, Gardner described *On Moral Fiction* as "an attempt to develop a set of instructions, an analysis of what has gone wrong in recent years with the various arts—especially fiction, since that is the art on which I'm best informed."[5] In it he offers several "Premises on Art and Morality," the chief of which are assertions that art should be moral, in the sense of life-affirming, and that criticism should judge literature in terms of its moral worth. But contemporary artists and critics, he goes on to say, are bothered by moral relativism and preoccupied with trivialities. Gardner himself insists that pluralism must be regulated according to human values; writers of fiction and literary critics should not allow pernicious works to exert their harmful influence on society. To employ one of Gardner's favorite metaphors: pluralism is no justification for allowing elephants to tromp on babies. His own commitment to a species of pluralism, however, prevents him from favoring the direct and authoritative interference with the elephant that promises the best hope of safety for the infant, for he is opposed to both censorship and didacticism, understanding by the latter term not simply works designed to instruct, but those whose teaching is heavy-handed and dogmatic.

Besides leaving unresolved the question of how to save babies without limiting the freedom of elephants, *On Moral Fiction* fails to cast much light on the religious dimensions of the problem. Gardner simply posits two alternative views of how ideals influence behavior, one grounded in a "religious" reading of the universe, the other in a "secular" one. Such a bifurcation of cultural realities tends to be accepted uncritically today, with the ethical consequence of making it appear that beliefs (and not just "facts," as certain philosophers have insisted) are somehow cut off from values, and therefore irrelevant to the quality of one's citizenship. Because Gardner implies that both "religious" and "secular" interpretations are equally valid (which is to say, impotent), he reduces the significance of belief in just this fashion. And, with such a division, he can only state the current dilemma; attempts to resolve it degenerate quickly into the "table banging" he warned readers to expect early in the book, when he declared, "I argue—by reason and by banging on the table—for an old-fashioned view of what art is and does and what the fundamental business of critics ought therefore to be" (p. 5).

But given Gardner's decision to divide things into the categories "religious" and "secular," his articulation of the dilemma is sound enough in terms of the ways Western theistic religiosity and atheistic (or agnostic) secularism are usually understood:

> If we agree, at least tentatively, that art does instruct, and if we agree that not all instruction is equally valid, . . . then our quarrel with the moralist position on art comes down to this: we cannot wholeheartedly accept the religious version of the theory because we are uncomfortable with its first premise, God; and we cannot wholeheartedly accept the secular version of the theory because we're unconvinced that one man's intuition of truth can be proved better than another's (p. 4).

Gardner leaves us, then, by his own admission, with no acceptable theory. Nonetheless, he continues to assert that his vision of what is good and true is superior to that offered by many other contemporary writers.

One might ask whether a broadening of the concept of religion would allow for a more penetrating discussion of the things Gardner wants to pursue. Is he not, after all, criticizing the beliefs embedded in fiction as much as the ways authors have drawn characters and related events? And is not the issue of what sort of attitude toward characters and events is true to reality basic to whether or not authors and readers can care about fictional persons in the way Gardner believes is necessary for "moral" fiction? Is it perhaps not the case that an uncritical commitment to tolerance has weakened our perception of the connection between belief and action? For if moral theory must prescind from the matter of religious belief (broadly understood), can the moralist be anything more than a cheerleader or a nag?

These questions touch more on matters of theology and ethics than they do on literary criticism. And this fact suggests that one of the reasons for the failure of *On Moral Fiction* to add much to our thought about literature and morality is the absence of disciplined theological and ethical reflection on the various forms of belief and value commitment or on the various possibilities of moral influence. Gardner, one may conclude, was a committed artist who lacked a theoretical language capable of articulating his intuitions about the importance of imaginative literature for life.

Whereas Gardner scolds and bangs on the table, Goodheart quietly laments the subject that is the title of his much more rigorous book, *The Failure of Criticism.* There he traces the lines of development leading to the current malaise, a criticism whose "moral sense of contrast has been severely weakened," a "liberation into plurality" that evokes "the emptiness of a game, not the rich-ness of human possibility."[6] He demonstrates the connection be-tween the loss of a central authority for critical judgment and the phenomenon called "secularization," noting that "questions about the moral authority of literature and criticism often turn upon a question of what happens when the sacred disappears or is sub-limated in the profane" (p. 7). Instead of proceeding to investigate the theological issues involved in modern religious experience, however, he describes recent literary-critical history in terms of a simplified dialectic between the "Catholic pessimism" of the moder-nists (Stendahl, Flaubert, Joyce) and the "Protestant optimism" of the English social critics (Carlyle, Ruskin, and Arnold):

> The feeling that the conversion of the inner man can possibly change the world and that literature can be an agency for such conversion is a phenomenon of modern English litera-ture from Carlyle to Lawrence and it is a phenomenon peculiar to the Protestant temperament. In contrast, the sen-

timent about the social powerlessness of art is a fact in the cultural life of Catholic countries.

Expressed as a virtue, the aesthetics of a Flaubert or a Baudelaire or a Joyce is a declaration of the purity of art, its freedom from contaminating moral and social concerns. As a vice, it is an expression of essential Catholic hopelessness about improving the world (p. 49).

This unsupported generalization seems a stop-gap attempt on Goodheart's part to account for a reality far more complex than anything that can be attributed to a "Protestant temperament" or a "Catholic imagination." Indeed, since he does no serious theological analysis, he would better have let matters rest with a more accurate statement he made earlier that the predicament of criticism can be viewed as "the expression of contending spiritual views of experience." But Goodheart is bent on distinguishing "the Catholic and Protestant energies of modern literature," an enterprise he bases on "the suggestion of Carlyle and Arnold that literature is a branch of religion" (p. 6).

Thus he finds that T. S. Eliot's "decayed Catholicism" undermines the critical potential he ought to have inherited from the great nineteenth-century English social critics. Eliot somehow belongs to that tradition, and his notion of culture is a reaction to Matthew Arnold's, but he lacks the confidence in the possibility of actually transforming society that Carlyle, Ruskin, and Arnold possessed in their "secularized Protestantism." Goodheart finds Eliot unable "to see society as a medium for the spiritual life" (p. 55), and judges his Christianity to be sectarian and ineffectual. He attributes to Eliot a "sentiment of resignation, verging on hopelessness, which is never fully admitted," and which is "a characteristic of the Catholic imagination" (p. 53).

The inadequacy of the Catholic/Protestant dialectic as a diagnostic device becomes quite clear in Goodheart's chapter on F.R. Leavis, the Cambridge thinker whose *Scrutiny* project and 1948 volume *The Great Tradition* had enormous influence on literary discussions and university curricula in the period after World War II. Leavis' "failure" cannot be attributed to Catholicism of any sort, for he inherited a Protestantism "akin to D.H. Lawrence's [that] moves him to search for spirit as an immanence in the world of time" (p. 76). But Leavis is not discussed in terms of confidence or lack of confidence in the will, the terms used to contrast "Catholic" Eliot with "Protestant" Arnold. Instead, Goodheart investigates Leavis' position more or less on its own terms and uncovers weaknesses that are both theoretical and temperamental.

Because Leavis had a strong bias against theory, his theoretical position must be inferred from remarks made in various contexts. Goodheart reconstructs it as one that equates "vitality" with the sacred and idealizes the "organic society," with its qualities of communal agrarian labor and "living speech." He criticizes Leavis' ideal of vitality as narrow and antiprogressive, and notes that his "conception of literature as *the* sacred milieu leaves him without resources when literature becomes profane" (p. 78). Most interesting in view of Goodheart's avoidance of his Protestant/Catholic dialectic in discussing Leavis, is the fact that he applies the same pejorative label to (Protestant) Leavis that he gave (Catholic) Eliot in the preceding chapter: "Manichaean." Faulting Eliot for a "self-impoverishing split between spirit and world," he had claimed that:

> [t]he Manichaeanism is not simply characteristic of *The Cocktail Party*, but is a governing principle of Eliot's imagination. And it is a feature of this principle that it refuses to allow the spiritual idea to fertilize the practical life, because it fears that spirit will be compromised and corrupted in the process. (p. 65)

Goodheart does not indicate how Leavis' "Manichaeanism" resembles or differs from that of Eliot, and indeed, he seems more to drop the term in passing than to apply it as a definitive judgment on Leavis: "Leavis' great tradition permits no alternatives. His Manichaean opacity to the evil Other is the price he has paid for his uncompromising conscience and his secure conviction." Eliot is

Manichaean, it seems, because of his tendency to reject the present world in favor of eternity; Leavis is Manichaean, perhaps by analogy, because of his tendency to reject modern literature, and indeed modern (chiefly urban) reality, in favor of the "great tradition," and a rural, organic way of life. Although the label "Manichaean" adds little to Goodheart's analysis, the fact that he introduces it as a category used by *critics* ("what certain critics have characterized as Manichaeanism," p. 65) is interesting in itself. By omission we learn that theologians are not part of this discussion, although the technical language of theology is employed to make a point. A theologian, of course, might have questioned the diagnostic value of the simplified Protestant/Catholic opposition from the start, and might perhaps have inquired why the more recent heretical label of "Jansenism" was not invoked in discussions of the authors from France and Ireland.

But isn't this cross-disciplinary nit-picking? Should not Goodheart be allowed to paint his picture of the failure of criticism in the broad strokes that help us see a pattern in the dismal scene? What justifies this preoccupation with theological "details," I submit, is precisely the excellence of so much of Goodheart's analysis, and especially his insight that religious matters are linked with the problem of criticism.

Goodheart rightly observes that the quest for transcendence and the need for salvation have not disappeared in the modern era. "The insistence on the autonomy of form," he notes, "presupposes a desire to discover in art a region of radiance and wholeness missing from modern life" (p. 112). This aspiration for artistic autonomy cannot be fulfilled, however, for it asks more than art can provide. The failed artist heroes depicted by Kafka, Mann, Proust, and Gide are for Goodheart "dramatizations of art's incapacity to save, however great its promise" (p. 166). He is convinced, in sum, that one of the factors contributing to the failure of criticism has been unrealistic expectations of art. Not surprisingly, his hope for a renewed humanist criticism hinges on a recognition of the limits of both art and criticism. "If criticism is to recover its powers," he maintains, "it must find its strength when it acknowledges the transcendence and mystery of grace" (p. 15). Goodheart seems to want to leave open some sort of theological alternative to the art-as-religion option and the "historicist's conflation of history and morality" (p. 19). He strongly objects to awarding history more authority than ideals, to acquiescing in the demise of humanism simply because it *seems* to have occurred.

Although he is definite about claiming that the obsolescence of humanism cannot be taken for granted, Goodheart hedges on the related question of whether theological claims can carry any weight against what Philip Rieff terms "the logic of secularization" (p. 103). In a chapter entitled "A Postscript to the Higher Criticism," Goodheart declares that Rieff has constructed an "intolerable dilemma" by characterizing the modern person as "Psychological Man," since "Psychological Man is the result of an irreversible desacralization, but man cannot survive without god-terms." At first Goodheart implies that by subverting "the logic of secularization" there is hope for a way out of this position, which would otherwise lead to "nihilism and moral suicide." In this vein he states that "the threat of nihilism may not be in the death of God but in the historical authority that gives this putative fact so much cultural power." But in the end he appears to accept this "putative fact" and join Rieff in articulating a hope that somehow god-terms-without-God can be relied upon to keep nihilism at bay:

> Without belief or a sense of purpose or a feeling of the rightness of things the instinct for survival has been known to disappear or disintegrate. In his confusion and uncertainty, Rieff may be hoping against hope that the destructive logic of secularization can be aborted by a sense of purpose that is at once atheistic and spiritual, so that the god-terms remain, confirming Proudhon's original sense of the "inescapability of religious language." Not exactly a gratifying situation, but there seems to be no other alternative at the present time (pp. 103-104).

Besides joining Rieff in an "intolerable dilemma," Goodheart appears thus to adopt a position with the same weakness he had earlier attributed to that of Matthew Arnold, namely, an inability to provide a grounding for moral authority. But Goodheart does not claim to supply a "way out." He has chosen here to recount the "failure" of criticism, and his analysis has been conducted not to provide a solution to the modern critical predicament, but simply to increase our understanding of this predicament and "to enlarge the territory of the discussion" (p. 7). In this he has succeeded to a considerable degree.[7]

Goodheart's metaphorical way of expressing this aim, however, gives me pause. In what sense does a discussion have territory? What is Goodheart getting at here? What have metaphors of place and space to do with "contending spiritual views of existence"? If we unpack this metaphor, I believe we shall discover that it is not helping us to recognize where we have "gone wrong" nor see how we can "do better," particularly where religion and literature are concerned.

II. Beyond Territorialism: Shifting Metaphorical Gears

The fact is that a great deal of talk about academic disciplines is based on an analogy, the idea that disciplines are like territory. It is a natural enough metaphor, and not without insight, but it has become so entrenched in our thinking that its limits and problems have escaped notice. We are not even aware of using metaphor when we say, for example, "my field is American literature," or "my area of specialization is philosophical ethics," but these expressions differ in important ways from observations like "I've got soybeans growing in that field," or the "area of a triangle is equal to the product of the base times the altitude." Jonathan Z. Smith has contributed a fine volume to religious studies called *Map Is Not Territory*, and someone would do well to follow suit with a book on the order of *Academic Disciplines Are Not Territories Either*.[8] The point is not trivial, for serious problems are associated with our common practice of thinking about disciplines territorially.

Just how common is this practice? Consider the title Robert Detwiler chose for a rich anthology of essays from Scholars Press: *Art/Literature/Religion: Life on the Borders.*[9] Or consider the religious variation on the territorial theme at the conclusion of Anthony Savile's recent review of Barbara Herrnstein Smith's *Contingencies of Value*, in which he faults the author for not attending to the "best current philosophical treatments of value," and expresses amazement "at the grievous lack of contact between neighboring parishes in the academy's supposedly integrated faculty of letters."[10] Who would argue with Ronald Green's assertion that we should recognize the "shared cognitive terrain" between ethics and science?[11] Doesn't Graham Hough ring true when he observes that [literary] criticism is constituted as a distinct field by having its centre in literature and its circumference on some not-strictly-definable line where literature ceases to be visible?[12]

Or does he? Hough goes on to say that "part of the territory so described [as belonging to criticism] is also occupied by other powers," and this phrase about the occupation of the critical "field" by other powers reveals one of the major limitations of the territorial "root-metaphor," namely its tendency to encourage a scholarly version of what theologian and critic of culture H. Richard Niebuhr called an "ethics of self-defense."[13] And, we might add, at times of aggression as well.

Academics devote an enormous amount of energy to self-justification and defense of their turf, and one wonders if the territorial root-metaphor for understanding the relationships among disciplines has something to do with this unproductive form of polemicism. Argument is surely at the heart of scholarship, but fighting about boundaries drains resources that could well be devoted to more pressing matters.

Where did Hough get this language of occupation by "other powers" anyway? A likely possibility is that Hough, who wrote in 1966, had been influenced by the 1957 study *Anatomy of Criticism* by Northrop Frye. This classic of mid-century literary theory was composed in the era of Sputnik and the cold war, and the territorial metaphor for understanding academic disciplines contributed directly to the tone Frye chose for his opening essay, which he entitled "Polemical Introduction." Frye saw that university funding was going to the sciences, and felt that if the humanities were not to wither and die, they would need to become scientific too. In particular, he perceived literary criticism to be in a besieged state, and proposed a "scientific criticism" to rescue the discipline. Note how the territorial metaphor has a tendency to make one eager for academic battle, as Frye depicts the situation in 1957: "It is clear that the absence of systematic criticism has created a power vacuum, and all the neighboring disciplines have moved in." Here Frye is adding to an argument he had advanced a few pages earlier in terms that display a sacramental faith in the power of something he called "science." Wrote Frye:

> The presence of science in any subject changes its character from the casual to the causal, from the random and intuitive to the systematic, as well as safeguarding the integrity of that subject from external invasions.[14]

Thus we see how territorial metaphors spawn military ones. What results is a preoccupation with battle that distracts us from what I take to be the true goal of criticism, namely, the understanding and assessment of literary texts, not the preservation of "territorial rights."

Another problem with the territorial metaphor is that it leads us to deal at most with two things at a time. By definition, only two entities share any given stretch of boundary. We are always at one checkpoint or another, theology at the frontier of literature, criticism crossing oh-so-gingerly the border of moral philosophy, terribly nervous about being caught in exchanges of value. For many reasons it has seemed risky enough to link literature with religion or morality, but rarely with both at once.[15]

And finally, there are institutional problems that the territorial metaphor sustains, and these need to be remedied. Gerald Graff's

recent account of academic literary studies in the United States
shows that the "field-coverage" principle of simply adding new
subjects to literature departments and stressing "productivity" in
isolated research areas prevents progress on points of significant
cultural conflict because, on the whole, specialists in one subfield
are not engaging those in others, much less dealing with the public
at large. According to Graff, ". . . the routinization of critical discourses is a function of institutional arrangements that do not require these discourses to confront one another."[16]

It is indeed a minimal concept of neighborliness that assumes we
only need "good fences" to make "good neighbors" in the academic
community. T. S. Eliot, who himself sought more conceptual clarity
about literature, morality, and religion than Matthew Arnold had
provided, was on to something when he testified:

> You can never draw the line between aesthetic criticism and
> moral and social criticism; you cannot drawn the line be-
> tween criticism and metaphysics; you start with literary
> criticism, and however vigorous an aesthete you may be,
> you are over the frontier onto something else sooner or
> later.[17]

When one reaches such an impasse, I would suggest, it is time to
reconceive the enterprise, and in this case it is high time to replace
the territorial root-metaphor. Or, if "replace" is too strong a term,
we could speak of shifting metaphorical gears or giving the territorial analogy a rest for the time being. The approach that views
the disciplines as geographical entities may have the advantage of
clarity, but this is gained at the expense of accuracy, and often also
of civic-mindedness and civility. The boundary disputes, defensiveness, and polemicism associated with the territorial metaphor
deflect attention from the objects we study, which always transcend
our maps of reality, and this territorial carving up ignores the facts
of our experience. When we read a novel or attend a play, what we
have is precisely *our experience* of the text or performance, which includes in highly-disorganized fashion aspects that can properly be

termed religious, moral, aesthetic, psychological, and so on, all more or less at once.

What then do I recommend, if the territorial metaphor has over-drawn its account? My proposal is that we conceive things in light of a *conversational* metaphor, which assumes that thinkers with different sorts of intellectual histories and institutional locations have useful things to say about problems of common concern, if only we can sit still and listen to each other. This metaphor fits well with the objects of study, literary texts, for as Gerald Graff rightly points out, "no text is an island." Rather, ". . . every work of literature is a rejoinder in a conversation or dialogue that it presupposes but may or may not mention explicitly."[18]

Moreover, the conversational root metaphor is inherently collaborative, and it can easily accommodate more than two disciplines at a time. Here the assumption is that different disciplines contribute perspectives and tools of analysis rather than control parts of the academic earth. This approach, I believe, is more likely to do justice to the complex realities involved, and to enable scholarship concerning the arts to pay heed to the wise observation Elder Olson made fifteen years ago in the inaugural issue of the journal *Critical Inquiry*: "We come to know more about art as we come to know more about life, and we begin to realize [art's] true importance only when we realize that, important as art is, it would not be so important if other things were not *more* important."[19] These more important things, I would add, are precisely those human, those moral and spiritual concerns that in so many cases motivate artists to create art in the first place. And because literary art is concerned with the whole range of human experience, including moral and religious experience, ethicists and theologians belong in the literary critical conversation. Theologians in particular have much to contribute, for they are heir to decades of twentieth-century discussion of the very matter avoided by most literary scholars in this period, namely the relationship between religion and morality. There is nothing like unanimity in what theologians have concluded from their deliberations, but the conversation has advanced considerably beyond the point at which it rested in the days of Matthew Arnold.

Theologians, however, are not always welcome in humanist circles, for theology has been perceived by many in the modern age—and not always unfairly—to be a controlling, unreflective discipline, one that attempts to exercise regal prerogatives in a democratic era. Nonetheless, it remains possible to view theology as something other than a deposed "Queen" of the sciences, eager to regain power over all that is said and done in the university.

In fact, H. Richard Niebuhr has argued convincingly that the role of theology in the contemporary period is to be "not queen but servant," and it is in this capacity of service to human understanding and well-being that theologians belong in the humanistic, and particularly the literary critical conversations.[20] This is especially the case if the theologians in question are trained not only in the particular language of their religious tradition but also in the more general philosophical language that attempts to account for human experiences of transcendence, value, obligation, faith, and meaning.

III. In the Tradition of Ignatius

To summarize the argument thus far, and make explicit more of its underpinnings: I began by indicating that all has not been well in the discussion about literature and values, pointing out by way of two illustrative critiques of literary culture from a decade ago that certain concerns of literary scholars involve topics that require illumination from specialists in religion and ethics. This led me to inquire why there has not been more collaboration among the disciplines, when clearly there are such close links between, for example, literature, religion, and morality. Without claiming a monocausal connection, I have suggested that part of the problem involves the way we think about the relationships among academic disciplines, which has been governed by a *territorial* root-metaphor. After pointing out certain limits of this metaphor—its tendency to promote defensiveness, its inability to accommodate more than two perspectives at a time, and its social institutionalization in the "field-based" approach to organizing colleges and universities—I have suggested that a change is in order, and recommended a paradigm shift, or at least a shifting of metaphorical gears, to a *conversational* metaphor for thinking about the disciplines.[21] From here I went on to claim that the theologian belongs in the humanist conversation about literature, not as "Queen," but as participant, and indeed, as servant.

It is in such a spirit of service that I conclude this essay with a brief reflection that seeks to shed light on the question of how we may "do better" than we have lately been doing where liberal studies are concerned. I aim to draw out some connections I believe are present between the humanist approach to literary studies and to education generally that I am advocating and the spiritual tradition of St. Ignatius. When I originally presented some ideas on the theme of this chapter at the Inaugural Conference of the Jesuit Institute at Boston College, my brief remarks followed the classic format of an Ignatian meditation, ordered around three "points" well-known to those acquainted with the Jesuit spiritual tradition: examination of conscience, companionship, and imagination.

(1) **Examination of Conscience.** Ignatius recommended that self-examination be practiced more than once a day. And he meant *examining*—not staying on the surface of awareness, but calling ourselves to attention when we would rather be eating or dreaming. Ignatius would ask us to interrupt our normal patterns of work and sleep in order to allow what is below the surface to emerge so that we can understand what is really governing our lives and then decide whether or not we want to continue our allegiance to this governing force. Most of what I have written above is the fruit of such an examination, an examen of metaphor, if you will.[22] I have concluded that a significant shift is needed if we are to get beyond the impasse of theory improvising on theory and spinning off into increasing heights of unintelligibility, something we ought to do in a world that could use more practical help from its better-trained minds. To question the reigning territorialism and individualism

(whether the solitariness of the "lone researcher" or the collective isolation of subgroups within the humanities) is the first step in the conversion process entailed by this "examination of metaphor." The second is to embrace an alternative model, such as the conversational root-metaphor and the collaborative style of work that it can promote.

(2) **Companionship.** The idea of a socially-related and responsible humanities faculty is hardly new, but it has lately been out of favor because of notions about the "autonomy" of literature and criticism and pressures for positivistic rigor in specialized "fields" of study, among other factors. There have, of course, been insistent advocates of ethical criticism throughout this century, as Wayne C. Booth reminds us in a magisterial study from 1988, *The Company We Keep: An Ethics of Fiction.*[23]

Drawing on insights from philosophy and the social sciences as well as on his background in literature and critical theory, Booth argues persuasively in *The Company We Keep* for once again relating literary study (rhetoric) to ethics and politics. The conversation metaphor figures often in this book, which Booth says could well have been entitled, "A Conversation Celebrating the Many Ways in Which Narratives Can Be Good for You—with Side Glances at How to Avoid Their Powers for Harm." The work is based on the idea that narratives influence us the way friends do, and Booth's sophisticated unpacking of the classic "books as companions" metaphor is well worth the study of any who are involved in liberal arts education. This seems especially true in a Jesuit university, for his emphasis on the experience and effects of companionship fits very well with the Jesuit tradition. As we know from the name given the religious order he founded, Ignatius was keenly aware of the importance of "the company we keep." Moreover, Catholic artists and theologians have also stressed this theme, most productively in our time, I believe, when they seek the company of Jesus in the "least" of his brothers and sisters, the victims of undeserved suffering. I am reminded here of Graham Greene's remarks upon accepting the Shakespeare prize from the University of Hamburg in 1968, when he declared that "the writer should always be ready to change sides at the drop of a hat. He stands for the victims, and the victims change."[24] In this respect, the writer's vocation is not unlike that of the theologian, or indeed, the ordinary Christian. As Matthew Lamb reminds us in *Solidarity With Victims:*

> *Vox victimarum vox Dei.* The cries of the victims are the voice of God. To the extent that those cries are not heard above the din of our political, cultural, economic, social, and ecclesial bickerings, we have already begun a descent into hell.[25]

If we do stand with victims, of course, we shall come face-to-face with evil, and we naturally resist attending to evil of the scope, intensity, and intransigency that abounds in our world. Elie Wiesel has recognized that we cannot contemplate evil in large terms, and has wisely recommended that we start by considering a single child's experience of it. His own autobiographical novel followed this principle, and *Night* has helped bring the incomprehensible fact of the Holocaust to the awareness of millions, eliciting ethical responses from many readers.[26] Likewise, the photo of one child in pain from napalm burns as she ran naked down a road in South Vietnam did much to turn Americans against our military involvement there.[27] And once again, in April 1989, a child victim was haunting my thoughts as I prepared to contribute to the Inaugural Conference of the Jesuit Institute at Boston College. After reading about Carmina Salcido in the morning paper, I found myself unable to shake the sense of appalling evil from my mind as I tried to focus on the possibilities of this new Institute. There was this image of a three-year-old waking up in a California trash heap beside her dead mother and sisters, remembering that "Daddy cut me."[28] The evil is unfathomable. Though her throat will heal, it is hard to see how she will find her way in the future other than through one of the false gates tried by various characters in Elie Wiesel's narratives of Holocaust survivors—vengeance, madness, or suicide.[29]

Such evil is beyond our ability to comprehend. Yet we should not simply declare that these things are mysteries, or instances of sin, as if that were enough by way of a response. If the cries of victims are the voice of God, then are the cries of this child asking anything of the Jesuit Institute at Boston College? As I pondered this question, I began to see lines branching out from the child in the trash heap, which connected her sufferings with other instances of evil that filled the news in April of 1989. One line touched the disaster in a Sheffield soccer stadium, where dozens of children and teenagers were crushed to death by a violent surge of spectators against a steel fence. And another stretched toward the Alaskan oil spill, with all the ecological and economic damage this has meant. Such evil has many causes, to be sure, but one factor is implicated in all three cases. It is alcohol abuse, a member of the chemical dependency family that ruins the lives of countless victims each year in our country and abroad. If the Jesuit Institute would focus on this complex problem in a creative way, I believe it could substantially lessen the evil that many suffer unjustly in our world.

Why not concentrate the Institute's resources for a time on the problems of substance abuse and chemical dependency? Why not attend in a new way to the complaints about drunken students, which have come down from the sixteenth century even to last weekend? Why not focus on this evil, which already connects campus issues with wider concerns such as racism, sexual violence, and economic injustice? The time is right, it seems to me, to spend some of the Institute's resources in a gesture of companionship with suffering victims, a gesture that may go far toward alleviating future suffering associated with chemical dependency. In speaking of resources here, I am thinking especially of the *human* resources available to the Institute, including people's expertise across a spectrum of disciplines, their generosity and dedication, and especially their creative imaginations.

(3) **Imagination.** Through following the *Spiritual Exercises*, I have long known of St. Ignatius' esteem for the imagination, but only after considering John Padberg's review of Jesuit history did I see how this aspect of Ignatian spirituality has borne fruit in past instances of remarkable Jesuit creativity.[30] And creativity is precisely

what is needed to address the seemingly intractable evils associated with chemical dependency. We know that doing more of what we have been doing is not adequate; these evils will not be substantially diminished by tighter legal controls, better extradition treaties, more arms for law enforcement officers, or new and larger prisons.

In the case of the problem of chemical dependency, we need to take the problem back to the drawing board, converse across disciplinary specializations, touch into all the causal factors we can think of, and dream of solutions that haven't yet occurred to any of us. I would like to see theologians and historians together probe our culture's ambivalence toward bodily pleasure and pain, for short-term pleasure and long-term pain are what chemical dependency is all about. I would like to hear biochemists and psychologists converse about the neurophysiology involved in allergies and chemical addictions, as well as in "positive addictions" such as meditation and aerobic exercise, and in that powerful experience of being "in the zone," when one is able to contribute a peak performance in a chosen endeavor. These are only examples; the conversation will have to be an extended one, and it must manage to stay focused on long-term objectives without feeling driven to produce answers before it is ready. What we need are creative solutions, and for these we must cultivate trust and patience, and liberate our thinking from the territorialism and the pressures toward conformity that are too well rewarded in the academy as elsewhere these days. The key to creativity is what is called "divergent-productive" thinking, a phenomenon that can never be forced, but one that can be promoted if we have sufficient respect for the human imagination to give it time, in good company, to dream, to "fool around" with ideas, to play with seemingly incongruent possibilities until the needed answer to the problem at hand is, in every sense of the phrase, graciously given.[31]

If you will forgive the trace of a territorial metaphor at this juncture, let me say that imagination is not only the *sine qua non* of divergent-productive thinking, but also the natural bridge that relates religion and the arts (as well as the other humanities and the sciences) and connects the university with the civic and ecclesial societies it serves. For the Jesuit Institute at Boston College to become another outstanding instance of creativity in the order's distinguished history, it will surely do well to cultivate that quality of imagination so central to Ignatian spirituality. Whether or not my candidate for "conversation topic" is chosen, I hope that some issue of social significance will engage these newly available resources. Clearly the task of higher education is to promote understanding of the world, but never understanding for its own sake any more than "art for art's sake." The point of understanding the world is so that we can change it for the better. And this will be *ad majoriem dei gloriam.*

Notes

1. For accounts of problems concerning these three cultures, one might begin with Terry Eagleton, *The Function of Criticism: From The Spectator to Post-Structuralism* (London: Verso Editions and NLB, 1984) and Gerald Graff, *Professing Literature: An Institutional History* (Chicago: University of Chicago Press, 1987) on literary culture; James T. Laney, "Characterization and Moral Judgments," *The Journal of Religion* 55 (1975) 405-14, on post-Kantian philosophical culture; and Gerda Lerner, *The Creation of Patriarchy* (New York: Oxford University Press, 1986) on patriarchal culture. For a recent analysis of American academic culture, see Burton R. Clark, *The Academic Life: Small Worlds, Different Worlds* (Princeton, NJ: Carnegie Foundation, 1987).

2. John Gardner, *On Moral Fiction* (New York: Basic Books, 1978).

3. Eugene Goodheart, *The Failure of Criticism* (Cambridge: Harvard University Press, 1978). Goodheart characterizes humanist criticism as caring about "the quality of life as well as works of art" and being "inspired by a positive order of values, nourished by a moral understanding of the religious tradition and by a profound appreciation of the works of art and intellect of past and present" (p.8). My own use of the phrase is similar; "humanist criticism" of literature entails an approach that *admits* to valuing art for

humanity's sake rather than simply for its own sake, in contrast to approaches that refuse to articulate commitments to values beyond art itself. This general use of the much-contested label "humanist" by no means rules out, on the one hand, affirming a transcendent Source of human values, nor, on the other, recognizing that there is a point to the postmodern critique of past forms of humanism. Nor need humanist criticism degenerate into a moralistic, utilitarian approach to art, though it sometimes does.

4. For rich discussions of methodological issues concerning pluralism and two disciplines central to this chapter, see Wayne C. Booth, *Critical Understanding: The Powers and Limits of Pluralism* (Chicago: University of Chicago Press, 1979) and David Tracy, *Blessed Rage for Order: The New Pluralism in Theology* (New York: Seabury, 1975).

5. Gardner, p. 4. Subsequent references will be made parenthetically in the text.

6. Goodheart, pp. 2, 4. Subsequent references will be made parenthetically in the text.

7. Goodheart has more recently published a brilliant critique of post-structuralist literary theory, *The Skeptic Disposition in Contemporary Criticism* (Princeton: Princeton University Press, 1984), in which he again adverts to the theological issues at stake in debates about literary theory. "Deconstructionists," he observes, "deny the faith, not from empiricist premises, but from a counterfaith in the void" (p. 37), an insight that reminds one of Paul Tillich or H. Richard Niebuhr. He again states the need to expand the "territory" of our concern (p. 38), insisting that the humanities must be related to "our political and moral lives" as well as our educational institutions. Although I resist the territorial metaphor in which it is expressed, I strongly agree with his basic point. Theologians ought, I believe, to draw the inference from what Goodheart says about deconstruction: "In accomplishing their feat, deconstructionists have not demonstrated the 'nothingness' that they say is present everywhere, but they require us to do what no one has yet ade-

quately done: to rearticulate the absent something that we continue to experience" (p. 30).

8. Jonathan Z. Smith, *Map Is Not Territory: Studies in the History of Religions* (Leiden: Brill, 1978).

9. Robert Detweiler, ed., *Art/Literature/Religion: Life on the Borders*, Journal of the American Academy of Religion Series, vol. 49, no. 2 (Chico, CA: Scholars Press, 1983).

10. Anthony Savile, "But Some Books Are Still Bad," *New York Times* (June 4, 1989) VII, 35:1.

11. Ronald Green, "Should We Return to Foundations?" in T. Tristram Englehardt, Jr. and Daniel Callahan, eds., *Knowing and Valuing: The Search for Common Roots* (Hastings-on-Hudson: Institute of Society, Ethics, and the Life Sciences, 1980) 278.

12. Graham Hough, *An Essay on Criticism* (New York: W. W. Norton Co., 1966), p. 6.

13. My use of the term "root-metaphor" (to characterize an image that governs thought and behavior, and is so common and so basic that it is rarely recognized as a metaphor) is indebted to H. Richard Niebuhr's discussion of "Metaphors and Morals," which draws on Stephen Pepper's book, *World Hypotheses*, and appears as an appendix to Niebuhr's *The Responsible Self* (New York: Harper & Row, 1963) 149-160. Niebuhr treats self-defensiveness in ethics on pp. 98-99 of the same volume.

14. Northrop Frye, *Anatomy of Criticism* (Princeton, NJ: Princeton, University Press, 1957) 12.

15. One obvious reason is the difficulty of "knowing the literature" of even a single discipline in a world of mushrooming publications, much less being conversant with that of two or three. There is considerable resistance to trading the individualistic research model associated with the humanities (does it derive in part from notions of the poet as divinely inspired?) for the collaborative

model that can better address complex questions. Joint authorship is common in the sciences, but rare in the humanities, though one hopes that such an excellent work as *Metaphoric Process: The Creation of Scientific and Religious Understanding*, co-authored by theologian and hermeneutical theorist Mary Gerhart and physicist Allan Melvin Russell, (Fort Worth: Texas Christian University Press, 1984) may inspire others to work collaboratively.

16. Gerald Graff, *Professing Literature* 243.

17. Quoted in Arnold Isenberg, *Aesthetics and the Theory of Criticism: Selected Essays of Arnold Isenberg*, ed. William Callaghan et al. (Chicago: University of Chicago Press, 1973) 265-66.

18. Graff, *Professing Literature*, p. 10. Graff goes on to praise the work of Robert Scholes, *Textual Power: Literary Theory and the Teaching of English* (New Haven: Yale University Press, 1985) for arguing that "to teach the literary text one must teach the 'cultural text' as well." He later cites the contributions of Mikhail Bakhtin on "dialogics" (as interpreted by Don Bialostosky) and concludes that "The pedagogical implication of dialogics seems to be that the unit of study should cease to be the isolated text (or author) and become the virtual space or cultural conversation that the text presupposes" (p. 257).

19. Elder Olson, "On Value Judgments in the Arts," *Critical Inquiry* 1 (1974) 90.

20. "Theology—Not Queen but Servant" is the title Niebuhr originally chose for an essay published in *The Journal of Religion* for January 1955. It appears under the title "Theology in the University" in *Radical Monotheism and Western Culture* (New York: Harper & Row, 1960), pp. 93-99. Here Niebuhr observes that theology is "first of all servant of God," but with other studies it is also "fellow servant of truth," with truth understood to be the "reflection of the nature of being itself" (p. 90).

21. My cautious language about "paradigm shift" here is influenced by Stephen Toulmin's persuasive observation in *Human Understanding: The Collective Use and Evolution of Concepts* (Princeton, NJ: Princeton University Press, 1972) that "paradigm-switches are never as complete as the fully-fledged definition (of an 'intellectual revolution') implies" (p. 105). I agree with Toulmin's point, and insist only that we be more conscious of our metaphors and utilize the best available for given purposes. Toulmin's critique of territorial thinking ("we must ignore contemporary attempts to divide off the various epistemic disciplines by academic frontiers with professional checkpoints" [p. 7]) has also influenced my thought, and I find his zoological metaphor for disciplines a productive one: "If intellectual disciplines comprise historically developing populations of concepts, as organic species do of organisms, we may then consider how the interplay of innovative and selective factors maintains their characteristic unity and continuity" (p. 141). For considering *interdisciplinary* relationships, however, I find the conversational metaphor even more helpful. For recent studies on "conversation," see David Tracy, *Plurality and Ambiguity: Hermeneutics, Religion, Hope* (San Francisco: Harper & Row, 1987), and J. Peter Schineller, SJ, "Conversation in Christian Life and Ministry," in John M. Lozano, CMF et al., *Ministerial Spirituality and Religious Life* (Chicago: Claret Center, 1986), pp. 91-116.

22. If St. Ignatius were alive today, I suspect he would be willing to examine some of his own metaphors, and perhaps to "deconstruct" the regal and military imagery he favored in the sixteenth century.

23. Wayne C. Booth, *The Company We Keep: An Ethics of Fiction* (Berkeley: University of California Press, 1988).

24. Graham Greene, "The Virtue of Disloyalty," in Philip Stratford, ed., *The Portable Graham Greene* (New York: Viking, 1973), p. 609.

25. Matthew L. Lamb, *Solidarity With Victims: Toward a Theology of Social Transformation* (New York: Crossroad, 1982) 23.

26. In an April 19, 1978 *Chicago Tribune* article objecting to the television mini-series *Holocaust,* Elie Wiesel declared: "Too much is there. The film is too explicit, too all-encompassing. The story of one child, the destiny of one victim, the reverberations of one outcry would be more effective—even from the artistic point of view." Wiesel's *Night,* translated from the French by Stella Rodway, was first published in 1960 (New York: Hill and Wang).

27. On Sunday, October 8, 1989, the *St. Paul Pioneer Press Dispatch* carried a syndicated story from the *Los Angeles Times* by Judith Coburn ("A Picture of Healing") following up on the child, whose two younger brothers were killed instantly in the 1972 bombing raid. The Associated Press photographer, Nick Ut, drove the injured girl to a hospital fifteen miles away (where she was treated for fourteen months) and stayed in touch with her family. Kim Phuc recovered sufficiently from her excruciating burns to be able eventually to study in Cuba, and in 1989 she plans to leave Cuba for six weeks to bring a message of "reconciliation" to the United States. Nick Ut, who left Vietnam in 1975, visited there for the first time in January 1989. He told Coburn that Vietnamese children are "still getting wounded by unexploded mines. There's not enough food, and no medicine," adding, "I took that picture, but children still suffer and there is still war."

28. For *New York Times* coverage of this case, see editions for April 18 and May 9, 1989. Carmina's father, Ramon Salcido, was apprehended in Mexico and charged with seven counts of murder and one of attempted murder.

29. See Irving Halperin, "From *Night* to *The Gates of the Forest*" in Harry James Cargas, ed., *Responses to Elie Wiesel: Critical Essays by Major Jewish and Christian Scholars* (New York: Persea Books, 1978), 45-82.

30. See Chapter I above: "Imagining a Heritage" by John Padberg, S.J.

31. On imagination, see Richard Kearney, *The Wake of Imagination: Toward a Postmodern Culture* (Minneapolis: University of Minnesota, 1988). On creativity and divergent productive thinking, see essays by E. Paul Torrance, Abraham H. Maslow, and others in Ross L. Mooney and Taher A. Razik, eds., *Explorations in Creativity* (New York: Harper & Row, 1967).

Speaking to Whom?

Denis Donoghue
The Henry James Chair of Letters
New York University

It is not my business, nor would I feel competent, to tell the members of the Jesuit Institute what they should be doing. Indeed, I have never taken the risk of saying, even to myself, what I am up to, or why I spend my time in one way rather than another. But I think the crucial questions arise not by asking "what" but rather "to whom." Let me put the matter as succinctly as I can. To whom do you regard yourselves as speaking? I shall go roundabout to explain the little I have to say.

In 1926, I. A. Richards published *Science and Poetry*, a brief consideration of literature and belief in the light, as it appeared to him, of modern science. Like Matthew Arnold, Richards took it for granted that religion, specifically the doctrines of Christianity, had failed, brought down if not brought low by Darwin and Higher Criticism. Like Arnold, too, Richards thought it possible that the emotional force of Christianity, or indeed of any of the major religions, might be retained even after the collapse of doctrine and dogma. The emotions could be housed in the form of poetry, released from dogmatic responsibility. The fundamental fact about the modern world, according to Richards, was "the neutralization of nature"; that is, the change from a magical view of the universe to a scientific view. Literature should now proceed upon the scientific assumption that the universe, such as it is, is neutral; it is not the repository of spiritual life or an excuse for loose emotions. If some writers, notably D.H. Lawrence and W.B. Yeats, still held to the magical view, so much the worse for them.

147

Like Arnold, again, Richards thought that poetry was fully capable of saving us, because it could exemplify the successful organization of our feelings and impulses: the poetic forms could respond to our feelings and enact a satisfactory degree of coherence among them. The achievement of poetic form corresponded to the achievement of an adequate degree of equilibrium. According to Richards, a great poem is a structure that organizes a large number of impulses and brings them into equilibrium. Short of such harmony, the impulses would be vagrant, chaotic, and would inevitably destroy one another in conflict. Reading a great poem is the experience, justly exhilarating, of witnessing an immense achievement of order. We see how impulses, in themselves so different as to bring the organism to a halt if left to their warring devices, are reconciled in the poem. The best poem is the most complex; not in the sense of "the most difficult," but in the sense of bringing to a state of equilibrium the most disparate and the most exacting emotions provoked by the situation at hand. The "interinanimation of the words" in a great poem corresponds to the complex relation between our many impulses, developed into coherence and order.

The model for this achievement, according to Richards, is the central nervous system in the human body. It is described, most persuasively for Richards, by C. S. Sherrington in his *Integrative Action of the Nervous System* (1906). "With the nervous system intact," Sherrington says, "the reactions of the various parts of that system, the 'simple reflexes', are ever combined into great unitary harmonies, actions which in their sequence one upon another constitute 'behavior'." A poem, in Richard's terms, is "a collection of impulses" brought, by the forces of diction, syntax, and rhythm, to the highest possible degree of equipoise, "an equilibrium of opposed impulses."

The point of this activity, according to Richards, is self-evident: if you can see it happening in a poem, you know it can be done. Instead of being the victim of my rowdy impulses, I can make sense of them, draw sense from their conflict. Even if I can't write a poem, I am encouraged by reading one to believe that I can cope with my impulses without having to suppress them. Richards' pupil, William Empson, put the matter clearly in *Seven Types of Ambiguity:* "The object of life, after all, is not to understand things, but to maintain one's defenses and equilibrium and live as well as one can: it is not only maiden aunts who are placed like this."

It is a complication, of course, that you have to do this while living; you can't take sabbatical leave and sort everything out in advance of particular needs: "It does not even satisfy the understanding," as Empson says, "to stop living in order to understand."

These considerations, and their bearing upon the question of literature and belief, drove Richards to distinguish, in *Principles of Literary Criticism*, between "scientific belief" and "emotive belief." Scientific belief "we may perhaps define as readiness to act as though the reference symbolized by the proposition which is believed were true." Emotive belief is a far more provisional relation of attitudes and feelings. It is not a belief that such and such is the case, but that "if things were such and such, then . . . ." In literature, music, and architecture, Richards maintained, "attitudes are evoked and developed which are unquestionably independent of all beliefs as to fact." T.S. Eliot's *The Waste Land*, for instance,—I take this passage from Richards' review of Eliot's poems in the *New Statesman*, February 20, 1926, which he added to the reissue of *Principles* in that year—contains many ideas, but the poetry of the poem does not depend on the truth of the ideas. "The ideas," according to Richards, "are of all kinds, abstract and concrete, general and particular, and, like the musician's phrases, they are arranged, not that they may tell us something, but that their effects in us may combine into a coherent whole of feeling and attitude and produce a peculiar liberation of the will." Richards didn't specify what form this liberation takes. Liberation from what? Presumably from the prejudices, fixations, and insistences which afflict us when our beliefs attach themselves to facts which are not facts at all or can't be proved to anyone's satisfaction. Reading *The Waste Land*, our minds engage in an extremely complex play of ideas and attitudes which are independent of our belief. Our will is liberated not merely by the play but by the balance of impulses the poem at last achieves.

It is clear from *Principles of Literary Criticism* and Richards' *Coleridge on Imagination* that Richards' theory of poetry comes as much from Coleridge as from Sherrington; and perhaps as much from Plato's *Phaedrus* as from the famous passage in the fourteenth chapter of *Biographia Literaria* in which Coleridge describes poetry by describing the poet:

> The poet, described in *ideal* perfection, brings the whole soul of man into activity, with the subordination of its faculties to each other, according to their relative worth and dignity. He diffuses a tone and spirit of unity, that blends, and (as it were) *fuses*, each into each, by that synthetic and magical power, to which we have exclusively appropriated the name of imagination. This power, first put into action by the will and understanding, and retained under their irremissive, though gentle and unnoticed, control (*laxis effertur habenis*) reveals itself in the balance or reconciliation of opposite or discordant qualities: of sameness, with difference; of the general, with the concrete; the idea, with the image; the individual, with the representative; the sense of novelty and freshness, with old and familiar objects; a more than usual state of emotion, with more than usual order.

It is substantially the same theory of imagination, except that Richards has given it an entirely secular character, removing the traces of Christianity which adhere to the *Biographia Literaria* as a whole. Richards has used Sherrington to give Coleridge's theory of imagination a ground in neurophysiology and a culmination in psychology.

It was Richards, more than any other critic in a literary context, who provoked the debate about literature and religion 60 years ago. In "A Background for Contemporary Poetry" (*The Criterion*, iii (July 1925)), he argued that it was now necessary, in view of the collapse of "the edifices of supposed knowledge," to order our lives upon different assumptions:

> A sense of desolation, of uncertainty, of futility, of the base-lessness of aspirations, of the vanity of endeavour, and a thirst for a life-giving water which seems suddenly to have failed, are the signs in consciousness of this necessary reorganization of our lives.

To that sentence Richards added a footnote which had consequences he could hardly have seen:

> To those familiar with Mr. Eliot's *The Waste Land*, my indebtedness to it at this point will be evident. He seems to me by this poem to have performed two considerable services for this generation. He has given a perfect emotive description of a state of mind which is probably inevitable for a while to all those who most matter. Secondly, by effecting a complete severance between his poetry and *all* beliefs, and this without any weakening of the poetry, he has realised what might otherwise have remained largely a speculative possibility, and has shown the way to the only solution of these difficulties. 'In the destructive element immerse. That is the way'.

Eliot was editor of *The Criterion*, so he could have intervened before the footnote was published. For whatever reason, he let it stand. He stayed silent on the matter when he reviewed *Science and Poetry*. But in "A Note on Poetry and Belief" (*The Enemy*, 1 (January 1927)) he dissociated himself from Richards' argument. "I cannot see," he said, "that poetry can ever be separated from something which I should call belief":

> As for the poem of my own in question, I cannot for the life of me see the 'complete separation' from all belief . . . A 'sense of desolation', etc. (if it is there) is not a separation from belief; it is nothing so pleasant. In fact, doubt, uncertainty, futility, etc., would seem to me to prove anything ex-

cept this agreeable partition; for doubt and uncertainty are
merely a variety of belief.

Eliot was now about to enter the Anglican communion, so it was an
urgent matter for him to make his position as clear as possible. To
his essay on Dante, published in 1929, he added a long footnote distinguishing his position, on the question of literature and belief,
from Richards', and adding this disclaimer:

> Mr. Richards' statement (*Science and Poetry*, p. 76 footnote)
> that a certain writer has effected 'a complete severance be-
> tween his poetry and all beliefs' is to me incomprehensible.

Finally, in one of the Charles Eliot Norton Lectures, at Harvard—
this one, "The Modern Mind," delivered on March 17, 1933—Eliot
came back to Richards' offending phrase, slightly but significantly
misquoting it:

> But what a poem means is as much what it means to others
> as what it means to the author; and indeed, in the course of
> time a poet may become merely a reader in respect to his
> own works, forgetting his original meaning—or without for-
> getting, merely changing. So that, when Mr. Richards as-
> serts that *The Waste Land* effects 'a complete severance be-
> tween poetry and *all* beliefs' I am no better qualified to say
> No! than is any other reader. I will admit that I think that
> either Mr. Richards is wrong, or I do not understand his
> meaning. The statement might mean that it was the first
> poetry to do what all poetry in the past would have been the
> better for doing: I can hardly think that he intended to pay
> me such an unmerited compliment. It might also mean that
> the present situation is radically different from any in which
> poetry has been produced in the past: namely, that now
> there is nothing in which to believe, that Belief itself is dead;
> and that therefore my poem is the first to respond properly
> to the modern situation and not call upon Make-Believe.
> And it is in this connexion, apparently, that Mr. Richards ob-
> serves that 'poetry is capable of saving us.'

The misquotation is interesting. Richards didn't say that *The Waste Land* effected a complete severance between poetry and *all* beliefs; but that Eliot in this poem had effected "a complete severance between his poetry and *all* beliefs . . . ." Richards seems merely to be saying: *The Waste Land* is a kind of poetry that doesn't depend upon Eliot's beliefs, or anyone else's; and that kind probably shows the only way forward, the situation of belief being what it is. I think, further, that Richards' sentence is more limited than Eliot's interpretation of it, in another respect. Richards seems to be saying that when you're reading a poem or listening to a symphony, you shouldn't let your system of belief intrude on the experience. The value of reading a poem is that it encourages you to think that your own feelings needn't stay a mess: there are resources for bringing them to harmony. I don't imply that Eliot would have been persuaded by this more limited version of the argument. How could he be, since he believed that "the chief distinction of man is to glorify God and enjoy Him forever?" In reply to Richards' assertion that poetry is capable of saving us, Eliot said that this is "like saying that the wallpaper will save us when the walls have crumbled."

II

In glancing at this exchange between Richards and Eliot, I am aware that there is much more to be said about it than I have offered to say. The questions at issue between them include these: the possibility of religious belief; the validity of Christianity in a world apparently dominated by scientific positivism; the bearing of religious belief upon author or reader in the transactions of reading; the possibility that an argument conducted by two people who differ so fundamentally may be incorrigible. I am not aware that these and other difficulties that might be mentioned in the same breath have been resolved in the 50 or more years since Eliot and Richards disagreed. So I revert to the first question I asked: to whom does the Jesuit Institute think it is talking? Do Jesuits assume that they are talking to T.S. Eliot in the years after his conversion, when he was the most determined advocate of what he called "a Christian society"? The idea of a Christian society preoccupied him and determined the direction of his work as poet and social critic from 1928 to virtually the end of his life. What form would a Christian society take? How should a Christian proceed in order to bring such a society about? Do Jesuits assume that these are the questions which should occupy their minds, and that they are addressing not indeed T.S. Eliot but people who would speak, if they could, in his terms? Or do they assume that the people they address are more accurately represented by the Richards of *Science and Poetry* and *Principles of Literary Criticism*?

A second question, issuing from the first: What attitude can the Jesuit Institute take to the fact that in the received discourse surrounding literature and art it is nearly universally assumed that no intelligent man or woman can retain a religious belief? It is deemed impossible for such a person to be a Catholic. If, with a contrary intention, one points to the fact that every Sunday, and not only in remote parishes in Ireland, the churches are crowded with believers, the answer is that these people must be fools or fanatics.

There is another issue, inescapable if we are teachers. What does reading entail? Richards was one of the most influential theorists of reading in his time and beyond it. *Principles of Literary Criticism* and *Practical Criticism* are the source of the New Criticism and therefore, till the present moment, of the standard procedures in undergraduate classes in the teaching of English throughout the United States. Mostly, what goes on in our undergraduate classes is close reading of a few texts. The method is practised for many persuasive reasons, including the fact that you can engage in it, as Richards did, without believing anything.

I do not object to our classroom procedures. Indeed, I wish we had more fully learnt Richards' lessons and could be satisfied that we have trained our students to command his skill. We could then go ahead and ask difficult questions about his interpretation of *The Waste Land*. What precisely did he mean by that famous phrase? What form did his reading of the poem take, such that it issued in the phrase as a conclusive gesture? What values are entailed by that reading?

I see no evidence that in our teaching we have engaged with such issues. My experience suggests, on the contrary, that we are teaching works of literature as mere pretexts for discussing their apparent contents. We teach *Othello* so that we can have a classroom conversation about prejudice, race, heroism, sexual jealousy. The fact that *Othello* is a play, and that these themes have become a form available to a distinct kind of perception which we used to call aesthetic seems no longer a consideration. The fact that prejudice and race could be discussed just as well by reference to *Mississippi Burning* or to no particular situation is, it seems to me, quietly ignored. A class is regarded as successful if there is a lot of talk in it. The play is not the thing.

Why should Jesuits, in particular, worry about these matters, which are—or should be—causes of concern to every teacher? No special reason, unless they think of themselves as talking to Eliot rather than to Richards. My advice is: assume that you are talking to Richards, and try to deal with the enormous problems entailed by that assumption. It is not a matter of urgency to mediate between Gadamer and Habermas: that is merely a matter of fine tuning. To intervene between Richards and Eliot—really to understand and cope with the conflict—is a more exacting task, and far more urgent.

Belief and Culture

Rosemary Haughton
Wellspring House, Gloucester, Massachusetts

There is an experience common to many people who were brought up in one of the traditional Christian churches and who have continued to struggle to be faithful both to their traditions and to themselves. It is the experience of discovering that religious idioms that once were adequate to express a lived personal reality have lost their truth-telling capacity and have become personally unusable. It can even become embarrassing to remember that one once used such language, and one hopes that friends may have forgotten, or perhaps share the same uncomfortable memories. Old letters touching on religious subjects, or the re-reading of once-favorite books, produce not nostalgia but irritation and amazement and even anger. How could I have accepted those things, expressed myself like that?

I am not talking about people who have "lost their faith," whatever that means. I am talking about people who find that faith can no longer be truthful in the terms that once seemed quite adequate. They are committed to their faith, but changes within and without make it impossible to accept a given formulation of faith.

This is not entirely a new phenomenon. There have always been some whose journey of faith brought them to a point—or several successive points--where the expressions of belief which had seemed appropriate and indeed immutable were found to be, in effect, untrue to the reality of faith. Most of these faithful ones from the past, of course, we shall never know about. If they survived the Inquisition or accusations of witchcraft, it was because they kept their discomfort to themselves and some trusted friends, or perhaps joined some group led by more public heretics to whose affiliations the chances of history gave the immunity of power, and allowed the development of a new language of belief, ready in its turn to produce its own crop of the disillusioned. The more eminent and remembered among those who made these major faith/language transitions are (according to how things turned out) recorded as heretics, prophets, mystics or eminent theologians (theologians, that is, before the days when theologians became, by definition, expounders of the status quo, interpreters of a deposit of faith expressed in a deposit of jargon).

Abelard, for instance, managed to introduce a new dimension of humanity into Christology, and died in his bed. Julian of Norwich got away with a theology of divine motherhood of great consistency and revolutionary implications, and was revered. Others were less fortunate. Those who, like Luther, had strong political (and therefore military) support, had the chance to develop not only a coherent theology but a structure to express and support it. Some, like George Fox and Margaret Fell, had no political support but survived persecution and drew thousands of followers because they spoke a language that was heard by many of the quiet ones, gradually creating their own deviant structure without actually displacing others.

Stable cultures of the past, especially cultures developed by the structural necessities of an agriculturally-based life style (even in the towns) developed a "matching" language of belief that expressed itself in symbols and idioms which reflected that unquestioned continuity. In such situations, experiences that could seriously challenge the adequacy of this common idiom may come to individuals, but if they do there is no alternative language easily available. A gradual withdrawal of belief may occur, and clearly often did, emerging as cynicism or anti-clericalism or personal eccentricity. In the Middle Ages, people could find a way to live aberrant spiritual awareness by going off on pilgrimage (if necessary to the Holy Land, which took years) or becoming a hermit or a wandering mystic. Such people could be both acceptable and wildly eccentric in their theology as long as they kept their verbal expressions of it sufficiently obscure. Medieval society, perhaps because of its extreme interdependence and "public" quality, had a great tolerance for eccentrics, which could include theological eccentricity as long as the eccentric didn't try to convert others.

In such a society, where commonality of religious idiom is taken for granted, private and unproclaimed deviance is no threat. It is unlikely to produce a conscious search for different expressions of faith because faith is equated with the given and accepted idioms, so to feel uncomfortable with it is likely to lead to the withdrawal from it in some way or other, rather than an attempt to replace it with one which seems more truthful to lived experience. It is interesting that a frequent exception to this tolerance of individual withdrawal in Europe (even as late as the eighteenth century) in cultures with stable and state-supported Christian traditions, was witchcraft. Ill-understood and distorted, as it became through the centuries, far from its roots in the "old religion" and lacking coherence or real historical memory, it still had the sense in the public mind of an alternative belief system, one with power and long tradition. In the later centuries it had become, through persecution and suppression, at least in part a religion of subversion and revenge rather than one of hope, but it was a real alternative, and it continued to attract a few women whose realization of the way in which Christianity despised and deformed their feminine gifts drove them to look for something else. This example indicates how the break with religious idioms which leads to the kind of personal rethinking and amazement at old ways with which I began, requires not only that the old language begin to feel inadequate but that an alternative langage be available, at least vestigially—or perhaps in embryo. Abelard, for instance, drew on the language of romantic love to bring newness to theological concepts. Renaissance thinkers, like Erasmus and Colet, had the classical Greek philosophies to draw on.

Clearly, the contemporary situation is very different from a past where a coherent alternative language was only exceptionally available to express the nature and meaning of those spiritual discontents. In our time, there is a tolerance of alternative languages, up to a point, but this is due as much to a failure to understand the profound implications of language structure for ethical and behavioral judgements as to any real openness to different expressions of inexpressible truth.

The limits of tolerance, and of any intelligent understanding of the function of symbol, were made clear in the furor in 1988 over the Bishop of Durham's remarks about the resurrection of Jesus. His own grasp of theological symbolic language did not appear profound, and in any case didn't seem sufficient to enable him to foresee reactions to the language he used, or to enable him to nuance it or even (it seems) to understand the problem, while his hearers, even less theologically sophisticated, seemed quite unable to grasp even the long-established and traditional uses of symbolic language in expressing faith.

The details of this stupid encounter are not important here, but the strong feelings which frequently surface when a churchman of importance at least appears to be denying some basic doctrine shows very well how much a traditional idiom is connected to the spiritual and psychological structures of security in the minds of believers. This is true even though (or perhaps because) they do not live in a society whose common language of faith is worked out in common social and judicial structures. In a world where values shift and slide, where little can be counted on and change seems to the traditionally religious always for the worse, the quasi-certainties of faith are even more important. (Hence, indeed the attraction of fundamentalist sects of all kinds, both old and new.)

In the musical *Fiddler on the Roof*, the very name of the show expresses the sense of the precariousness of a group dependent on the whims of distant, uncontrollable and incomprehensible powers, and the importance for such people of cultural and religious "Tradition," to hold together the fragile strands of sanity, endurance and a tough kind of happiness. It is like a "fiddler on the roof," perched precariously aloft, but persistently playing a tune everyone knows so that all may continue to dance the measures and patterns of their identity and commonality, and find hope in that. The whole story shows the gradual stretching of the cultural web of identity, to points where it threatens to break, yet in the end it is strong enough to provide a new beginning in a strange land. This is only possible because of the persistence of the common symbol-system, and it shows why that matters, and therefore why it is always so threatening to the group and so frightening to the individual when the validity of the idiom is challenged, whether within the mind or from something outside.

So we find ourselves, in the West, in a cultural situation where there is no basic commonality of religious idiom, and yet where the need for the support it can provide is greater than ever. The present generation of believers is forced either to be aware of the fundamental inadequacy of language to convey ultimate truth—or to build psychological mechanisms which enable people to deny this.

A generation of philosophers and theologians has forced on us the realization that language in relation to reality is mutable, relative and culturally derived. In our own culture, to take a very basic instance, we give value metaphorically to experiences and persons by relating in terms of level and/or movement between levels: "higher" or "lower," "up" or "down." This is so ingrained in our language that it requires a huge mental effort in itself to realize that this is an arbitrary bit of symbolism, and not the only possible way to perceive, categorize and relatively value our units of experience. (We could, instead, think of things as "nearer" or "further," or "hotter" or "colder," for instance, which in each case would involve an interesting moral shift, because the differences would be clear but without necessary implications of better or worse. We could even classify by color.)

Even for those who do not read theology or philosophy, the effects of the undermining of given meaning are present, and have a profoundly disintegrating effect. Indeed, the theologians and philosophers themselves were only responding to the loss of meaning they perceived as already at work in the lives of ordinary people, and experienced in themselves. The rise of the "drug culture," the "me generation," the alienation of minorities—who develop their own cultural language to the point where they can no longer hear, or be heard by, the dominant culture—all these are aspects of the underground awareness so that nobody can be quite sure that they know what they mean or understand the meaning of others.

In the struggle to be in touch with this pervasive anxiety and its consequences, Boston College itself has provided a place where two major contributions to understanding and confronting the problem have been able to develop. One was the ground-breaking work of Bernard Lonergan, painstakingly teasing out the implications of how language is used, to bind and to loose, to explore and to conceal. The other has been Mary Daly, whose violent challenge to established modes of patriarchal thought has made it impossible for certain kinds of oppressive language usage to retain their former sense of inevitability and absoluteness. Because of these two, religious idiom and cultural experience are now obliged to be seen in relation to each other as they have never been before.

Because of such work, believers are now obliged to free imagination in a new way. As long as given symbols and metaphors for dealing with reality were unquestioned, imagination was in a coma. Now she has woken, and is lively and dangerous. All kinds of disciplines once assumed to be irrelevant, if not antagonistic, to religious thought now claim a part in shaping the idiom of belief because they themselves embody a language of reality. Though not new, quantum physics and systems theory have begun to provide new language and concepts whose implications have, in the last two decades, become important to theologians and religious thinkers. As old language certainties were shaken by the impact of two world wars, "the bomb" and the failure of Enlightenment optimism generally, these explorations provided new realism of imagination and symbol. They challenged the inherited language of belief which grew out of an Enlightenment categorization of human or non-human, "light" and "dark," real and unreal. At the same time, the urgency of a public ecological awareness if the planet is to survive, together with the literally different "point of view" of photographs of earth from space, and the vast mourning process which is beginning for irreparable destruction of our fragile home— all this has virtually destroyed the man-centered theology of the past. The women's movement has put the language of human dominance in the dock, accused of genocide, and has also challenged traditional separation of intellectual disciplines, and dualisms of "pure" and "applied" thought. It has done in reality what Jung proclaimed in the symbol of Mary's Assumption: raised the power of the right-brain, the feminine, up from the unconscious into the daylight of public and religious discourse.

All of this has happened more quietly and more powerfully than would have been possible before because of the communication explosion and the creation of the "global village." (This phrase, though originally a useful way to create awareness, is actually a mystifying misnomer, because a village is a symbol of stable interdependence, with a built-in resilience for dealing with crisis. A world united by communication is a world bewildered by its own conflicting data, competing ideas and unchannelled feeling, and rocked by the fear that every new crisis will destabilize its fragile system of competing composite egos.) The rapid communication of insights has also made people aware of many strands of experience and ways to express them which touch directly and indirectly on thought already being developed. So the process is very complex, and everyone concerned has the sense of something forever growing and changing in which we are caught up as it feels out new directions.

The result of all this is that believers who, even ten years ago, were pushing ahead in their own areas, challenging, forging new language, opening up new vistas with a kind of excited carelessness, are now more sober. They are more aware of the nature of what they have stirred up, and of the tremendous importance of this work for the threatened human race. They understand better just how difficult their task is, and how vital, if human freedom and compassion are to endure at all. There is an awareness of the kind of thing I began with—that is, the fundamental importance for human survival of secure symbol-systems that give identity—and yet the knowledge of how fragile these are; so the task becomes a search for a deeper level of religious identity, grounded in enduring symbol but able to live with the mutability of the interpretation of symbol and the constant deconstruction and reconstruction of language. This process was once so slow that nobody noticed, but now it can be observed and documented. The T.V. series, (published as a book) on "The Story of English" illustrates very well how language changes with cultural and economic change, and how it changes and is changed by moral and ethical experiences. The new mood of sobriety in exploring the implications and possibilities in shifting symbol-systems, and a sharp focussing of purpose in consequence, has been given extra urgency by the strong emergence of the "other" way of dealing with the changes in the perception of the relation between belief and culture: this is a stampede back to the fort and a closing and barricading of the gates of orthodoxy.

This is the way chosen by many believers who feel their group identity being undermined by the questioning and the language shift following major cultural change. The "fundamentalist" systems, both Christian and Islamic, are obvious examples, but the Roman Church is, at this time, clearly responding in a similar way. Its response to the impact of experiences that change the cultural landscape is, in a sense, to remove the area of debate "off the ground," out-of-reach of earthly challenge. In other words, its strategy is to re-establish a dualism that makes it possible to speak a language of belief that has little contact with the language of everyday concern.

This dualism keeps carefully separate, as always, the political and the religious, the sacred and the secular, the spiritual and the material. Words like "sacrament," "heaven," "holy," and, of course, "Jesus" are used to separate belief from culture.

Abstract and highly-professional theological jargon is easy to keep under control. One way to keep it abstract is to use language that once reverberated with the emotional experiential commitment that went into forging it to express profoundly-felt reality, but which has long lost contact with the experience. But there are important exceptions to this separation.

These exceptions have to do with the need to establish that control over people's everyday lives which is precisely what has been threatened by the tendency to explore and re-define critical areas of human experience, as the experience demands and not as the leaders—functioning as symbolic centers and articulators of unity—decide to allow. The necessity for both the idioms which are abstracted, and for the exceptions which actually become more humanly particular (as we shall see) are rooted in a deeply-felt need, and the issues are sensitive and complex because, as we have seen, the strength and endurance of a symbolic system is absolutely necessary for the survival of group identity in periods of upheaval. The desire to maintain this unchanged, at all costs, and by any means easily appears to believers as the primary religious task, and especially so to the leaders of a group. By the same token, if the leaders consciously take on this task and proclaim it, they can count on a strong emotional response and support from many of their followers, frightened as they are by the insecurity surrounding them, and longing to be told that they need not fear. But the sincere belief that the situation calls for unyielding resistance to what looks like change (but which of course may actually be the real continuity, given the change in language values which happen, unnoticed, as time passes) is compounded by the inevitable fear of loss of power. The corruption that results from the exercise of power with minimal accountability then adds to itself the belief in the need for maintenance of unwavering "orthodoxy." The result is one of those waves of siege hysteria and righteous pursuit of potential traitors which has marked the history of major religious traditions, including even, in a mild way, such pacific groups as the Society of Friends and the Mennonites, but shows itself fiercer and more horrible in the case of large groups with real worldly power. The archetypal repressive system, the Inquisition, was of this kind, and the present regime in Iran is precisely similar in motivation and execution, including its fear of women. Less bloody, but clearly of the same kind, is the present "crackdown" of the Roman system, which also manifests a fear of women and what they represent.

This is not accidental. The "exceptions," (to which I referred above), to the dualistic response to cultural change which seeks to remove religious symbol-systems from contact with experiences which could call them in question, have to do with the need to maintain control over the minds and hearts of believers, and the areas in which this control is most at risk are those of leadership, and of sexuality and family systems.

It is comparatively easy to ensure orthodoxy when dealing with such doctrines as the Incarnation or the Sacraments by dealing with them in a spiritual area untouched by changes in cultural attitudes or in the relationship between language and concept, but when it comes to making political or family/sexual choices, the need for control has to deal with very concrete cultural situations.

In the area of leadership, the issues are clear. The suspicion of any political involvement by believers is natural enough. "Political" for this mind-set, means any movement or system which involves challenging an established hierarchy; it ceases to be regarded as "political" when it involves supporting and obeying that hierarchy, even when the hierarchy is secular. This is because the maintenance of any rigid governing structure helps to discourage the kind of questioning which also leads to a questioning of religious leadership. So at this point the religious system is indeed rooted in practical, earthly decisions. (Sometimes, the Vatican system has manifested a genuine concern for the plight of the poor under rigid governing systems maintained by the rich, but this concern confines itself mostly to exhortation to the rich and denunciation of misuse of power, seldom to questioning the structures of power themselves, or challenging the particulars of actual systems which enrich the few at the expense of the many.) The demand for control of seminaries and the harassment of "political" clerics is all part of the need to maintain strong control which is, of course, actually political control.

This area of involvement with concrete earthly system overlaps with that of sexuality and family choices. The traditional family structure is patriarchal in the simplest sense, and its maintenance helps to underpin the overall patriarchal control of the church. Feminism is consequently an obvious danger. More deeply, there is the need, so old that its rationale is no longer overt, to maintain the patriarchal system of inheritance, which requires legitimate heirs. It therefore involves a sexual double-standard, the subjection of women, and the outlaw status of all sexual relationships which threaten legitimate patriarchal succession, whether they be homosexual or extramarital heterosexual ones. This practical stuff of male power and inheritance is so well buried that even those who oppose Church attitudes in these areas are often driven to oppose them on other grounds, but the old unconscious fears are still the driving power. Such unions are described as "contrary to God's will" and "unnatural" because they interfere with the maintenance of patriarchal control, and patriarchal control is the practical expression of left brain dominance. It is the expression of the need to order, to contain, to keep control, and perhaps emerges from a primitive fear of the mysterious power of nature which man must resist and contain if he is to survive. The later history of Western culture is the history of the attempt to establish the left brain awareness as the only truthful one, relegating right brain function to the realm of dreams, fantasy, superstition in religion and women. The Church, guardian of mystery, is bound to be the structure most mortally afraid of those who actually feel comfortable with mystery, to the point of seeming to de-mystify it. To a left-brain control-system, mystery must remain in a separate realm to which the left-brain system allows limited access. The right-brain, the feminine, always threatens to break out and make it accessible in an everyday way.

An example is the phenomenon of Lourdes. Here, a girl child's mystical experience broke down the barrier to mystery, and threatened to allow ordinary believers unlimited access to the heart of the belief system. The response was masterly. The desire was channelled, controlled, and compelled into established categories of belief. The mystery still drew, and draws, its hundreds of thousands, but they are told exactly where to go, what to do there, and above all what to believe about it all. So what threatened to be a spiritual revolution was turned into the church equivalent of bread and circuses to satisfy the hungry poor.

It was no accident that Bernadette and her Lady were both female, and that the panic reaction against the effect of cultural change includes the exclusion of women from positions of influence in the church, but especially from those that touch the symbolic system in its sacred stronghold of liturgy, so that even little altar girls, or female readers, or women having their feet washed on Holy Thursday, become a genuine threat. Similarly, women must not teach in seminaries. In Iran, women who are not totally submissive are taken to concentration camps for punishment and "retraining." The logic is the same, though more complete political control allows more drastic measures.

Underlying all this is the fear of the right-brain function, always associated with the feminine. The right-brain is the traitor within the gates. It is the function that side-steps control, explores and envisions and makes connections. It is the function that enables symbolic systems to work. This is why it is so dangerous.

What is going on in times and places of major cultural shift is that the left-brain analysis is unable to deal with the new data. It has no categories for them, no defenses against them. What I have been sketching above is the two kinds of responses of belief systems to cultural upheaval. On the one hand is the attempt of the right brain to break out and discover ways of experiencing, conceptualizing, expressing and structuring reality: all of these except the first involve the left-brain as auxiliary—but never in total control. On the other hand, there is the panic attempt of the left-brain to maintain its own total control by pretending that disturbing right-brain input is irrelevant and cannot touch eternal truths, or else is evil and must be suppressed.

If one adopts this latter point of view, the issues are at least apparently simple. For the believer who is struggling to discover a truthful response, the decisions are far from simple. In a sense, all the decisions are as provisional and mutable as the symbol-systems they seek to incarnate. It is rather like trying to find one's way through strange country in a fog. Landmarks are invisible, signposts unreadable, but there is a path, and every now and then the fog thins and reveals a bush or a tree or a ruined cottage, or even the outline of hills ahead, and one moves forward, trying to interpret what is visible and choose the right way.

The problem is that we are trying to discover a religious idiom that is true to the continuity, as well as the newness, of human experience and that recognizes particularity but also universality in religious experience and expression. We have some words—old words which carry the emotional charge of their long history, and which refer to reality—but what kind of reality? If we are not prepared to avoid the dilemma by the dualistic method of "spiritualizing" the idiom of faith and removing it from experiential accountability, then we have to be prepared to allow the words to discover themselves in our lives, our loves, our plans, our families, our history, our political situation, our mystical insights, our inheritance of a great tradition. We have to learn to let the right-brain teach us to read the signs, but hold it accountable to left-brain observation and honest interpretation.

How can we find a way forward? A university is supposed to be the place *par excellence* where such a search can be conducted, yet in the present situation it is probably among the least able to do so. The sources of its funding, the family backgrounds of most of its students, the career-structures to which students direct their studies and the career-structure of academic life itself, are all patriarchal structures with a strong interest in preserving a dualist interpretation of the relationship between culture and belief. In a sense, the very existence of the university (virtually *any* university) depends on the continuity and approval of a social, economic and political system which is patriarchal, elitist and also paranoid (fearing the right-brain traitor within, as I suggested earlier). Never mind whether the secular administration of a nation is capitalist or socialist or just plain old dictatorship—the same basic structures operate. In the case of a Catholic university, the problems are compounded and the search for new directions made even harder by the religious validation of secular dualism and pseudo-patriotism.

The paradox is that the same Catholic tradition which seeks to limit and restrain symbolic imagination contains within it the motivation to break out and away, the commitment to truth at all costs, and—underlying all that—the centuries-old tradition of aesthetic, affective, mystical and symbolic expression. The right-brain traitor, in fact, becomes the savior; our Lady Holy Wisdom can provide a lamp in the gloom. She has sustained the possibility of truth, beauty and goodness through all the centuries of oppression and against the stifling power of institutionalized stupidity and insensitivity, always finding hands and voices to serve her and proclaim her, even at great cost. Stephen, Perpetua, Hildegarde, Hilda, Eckhardt, Francis, Julian, John Ball, Erasmus, George Fox and Margaret Fell, Shaker leaders both men and women, Sojourner Truth, Bernadette, Friedrich von Hügel, Dorothy Day, thousands more and many still living, have responded to a vision too deeply truthful to be codified, yet responsive to a shared tradition, able to use its idiom and to be heard. Each one shifted the symbols at least a little, each one directed the light, as it were, through a different-colored glass. Each one witnessed, sometimes to death, to the possibility of affirming faith through truthful expressions of belief rooted in the culture, yet producing flowers not expected, different yet clearly derived from the same vigorous stock.

There are ways to continue to draw on this deeper tradition, ways which are appropriate to a center of study, in that they happen best at a place of intersections, a meeting ground of gifts, ideas, traditions, disciplines. There are ways which, for their development, depend on flexibility of minds, courage of heart, and a willingness to notice, take seriously, and validate the unexpected, the things seen out of the corner of the eye, the oddity occurring in the course of the pursuit of the ordinary, even in notions and visions clumsily or extremely expressed which yet contain a hint of something real and worth exploring. This kind of awareness requires a humility that, theoretically at least, belongs to fine scholarship; it also requires faith in the possibility of human encounter with the divine— and the divine is notoriously idiosyncratic in its manifestations.

The enterprise, the never-ending human enterprise, is the discovery of Wisdom—who is truth, who is the Word, who is incarnate. Using the symbol, "Word" reminds us at once how baffling a quest this will be, for during most of the millennia of human existence on the planet there were no "words"; words as units of communication are products of literacy; what precedes and underlies words is the human presentation of purpose and intent in verbal form, as when "I give my word," a gift of truth in personhood. Remembering always that the Word is incarnate in many ways, we venture in imagination and come into the paths of Wisdom. The enterprise has to be carried on in unpredictable and dislocating ways. A certain amount of ground-clearing has to be done with traditional scholarly tools, appropriate mainly to make clear what we are not looking for: logical certainty, a final conclusion, a closed and manageable verbal theological system. We shall also continue to need the tools of analysis to critique and evaluate, to pick out the fine flowers from the weeds which grow so thickly (which are, after all, the "ancestors" of the flowers). But, for the most part, the task consists in providing favorable conditions and situations for Lady Wisdom to reveal herself.

We are dealing with the categories of the prophetic functions, which were explored with such insight by Walter Brueggemann some years ago. Prophecy is the right-brain function most clearly related to the work of Wisdom, and itself involving gifts traditional to the fullness of the faith tradition, such as visionary power, mysticism, healing, artistic creativity, the ability to find appropriate symbolic forms to convey experience. Brueggemann's twin tasks of the prophetic are, on the one hand, denouncing, criticism, grief and anger, and on the other announcing, visioning, energizing, creating new possibilities. And both of these tasks are grounded in memory: memory of how God has acted through events and people, and therefore can act again.

The Hebrew prophets recalled the earlier history to validate their denunciation and give symbolic power to their vision of newness. So did Jesus, and so have the prophetic figures of Christian Wisdom, whether their prophecy was primarily (though never entirely) in the form of words to be proclaimed and to rouse, or in the form of actions: those that denounce by making evil visible in succoring the poor and oppressed, leading an attack on the centers of oppression, and those that announce by visibly developing new ways of being and relating.

So the work involves telling stories, which means mostly retelling stories—old ones and new ones. We can tell a national story, as in Howard Zinn's devastating "A People's History of the United States," which shows up the greed and self-interest underlying the foundation of America ("liberty" confined to white upper and middle-class property-owning males). We can retell group stories, as we open up the early histories of many religious orders and movements, and discover both unexpected good and unexpected evil. We can retell personal stories, as when abused women learn to tell their histories in terms of oppression and survival, redefining the old interpretation that attributed the fault and the inadequacy to them. Doing this, we release the power of Wisdom in ways that can be emotionally and politically catastrophic—or rather, to use Tolkien's word, "eucatastrophic," a breaking down of the false and a breaking out of the truth. In doing this, words are changed, attitudes are transformed. This is political dynamite. To do this work in such a way as to allow the true things to discover themselves, rather than just explode, we need skills—skills of historical and psychological analysis, skills in group dynamics and in linguistics. We need the left-brain skills to sift, claim, and proclaim that which the prophetic power has released. And we need a lot of political awareness and experience, too, for the truth discovered to become part of an ongoing process of change; the task of Wisdom is not only to see the vision but to discover ways to institutionalize it appropriately, and so to allow it to grow.

But also resulting from the storytelling is a great surge of anger and grief. There is, now, a rising wave of such anger and grief throughout the world, as stories are told of political killings and torture, the degradation of women and children in all countries, the distortion of human minds, the destruction of the millennial riches of the planet and its creatures. Astronauts who have looked down on earth from space have told us how they wept at the signs of an increasingly sick and perhaps dying planet; at the same time Jonathan Kozol has told the story of how he wept with and for the homeless families crammed into rat- and dung-ridden Welfare Hotels in New York, where the bodies of children who die there for lack of good food and medical care are buried in mass graves on a prison island, and their parents may not follow them even to that grave.

Quite spontaneously, a kind of public mourning has begun to be done, and this is surely the work of our Lady Wisdom, whose child, Jesus, wept and raged over the suffering of his people, both at that time and in time to come. "Weep for yourselves and for your children," is a command laid on the women, representatives of the right-brain function, who know that before there can be healing there must be the anger at evil, the grieving for what is killed.

Then there is the delicate task of discerning the transition from grieving to healing and newness. To seek escape from pain in the frenzied activity of rebuilding is to build on crumbling foundations, but in a sense the task of creating alternatives is part of the grieving—or happens with it. In shelters for abused women, for instance, there is anger and grief, there is the motivation to denounce and expose the evil, and demand redress. At the same time, in order for a full telling of the stories to be possible, in order that an adequate language of sorrow be forged (breaking out of the old attribution of guilt, the old fatalisms) it is necessary for there to be (or quickly come to be) a very different kind of social atmosphere in the shelter. There has to be a way of relating and organizing the common life which is very different from the systems of control and domination which have condoned or encouraged the abuse in the first place. So the two go together, and the retelling of the stories and the analysis of them require new kinds of skills, to observe, to conclude, to apply.

Singing is important. There is a level of energy and courage which requires music to interpret and release it, and all movements of change have had their songs. They range from very simple chants that can gather a hundred thousand voices with one proclamation of commitment and hope, to complex and sophisticated music. Paul Winter's "Missa Gaia" has become for many a place of transition, as it expresses the human earthly involvement, the repentance, the pain, the hope, the praise, in sounds ranging from the howl of the arctic wolf to Gregorian chant. It is the voice of Wisdom crying out in her creatures. In a very different way, Webber's "Requiem," (derivative as it is in some ways, flawed by its pretentions yet nearly redeemed by its desires) at one point seems to express the whole poignant and yet confident cry of humankind to the one whom Julian called "our tender mother Jesus," as, in the "Pie Jesu," the voices of a woman and a child soar together in a plea for mercy and for peace. Without music of mourning and hope and courage, there can be no newness, and what it can do—Paul Winter's music does it amazingly well, as do some popular singers—as to evoke symbols which are trans-cultural. Music and song can allow symbols with traditional roots to be reclaimed and renewed, for instance in the song "Bread and Roses," which was written for the strike of women mill workers in Lawrence, Massachusetts in 1912, and carries all the marks of its time, yet manages to take on a new resonance in the voices of the century's last decade. Music, the original and preliterate vehicle of common memory, is still the art that can carry the Word beyond and before words.

Another point of transition from mourning to healing was created in the visual arts by Judy Chicago's extraordinary exhibit called "The Dinner Party." This is a display of 33 large ceramic plates arranged on embroidered runners on a vast triangular table, and each plate and runner expresses the personality, role, style and significance of a woman who somehow changed the history of her time and left a legacy of story-power for other women and all people. (Interestingly, several are Christian saints and mystics— Bridget, Hildegarde, Hroswitha and others.) The exhibit was denigrated by the artistic establishment because it did not fit the expected categories. Neither "art" nor "craft," it drew together many skills and was made by a large group of people with diverse talents. It drew on many levels of symbolism (not all equally successfully evoked, by any means) and shocked some by its clear feminine sexual symbolism. (As a culture, we are accustomed to phallic symbols, but disturbed by the symbols of female sexuality.) It was hard to find museums willing to give display space, yet people flocked to see it, and the atmosphere in the hall where it was set out was more like a cathedral than a museum. There was a feeling of awe, of the presence of intense emotion, and also of peace and satisfaction. Some wept, couples whispered gently, some stood still for long periods in quiet contemplation. For women, and many men, it was a prophetic statement. It called to anger and grief at what had been done to women, it called to vision and energy because of women's courage and achievement. It is a symbol of transformation, and as such aroused hostility and contempt as well as amazement and hope. In a more "vernacular" idiom, but like it in spirit and power, was the "Ribbon," the idea of one woman which led groups all over America, from homes to schools to prisons to hospitals, to embroider pictures and symbols of the beauty they did not want to see destroyed in nuclear war. Sewn together, the "Ribbon" was carried to and encircled the Pentagon five times on a day of prayer and celebration. (It was predictably ignored by the media, which soon after reported, at length, a protest of farmers with a procession of tractors.) The huge quilt commemorating AIDS victims was a later work of the same significance and transforming power.

It is important to explore the meaning of such events and such makings, for these push at the boundaries of verbal language, using symbols to develop meaning systems that cannot be worked on directly, but silently "grow" as they are used differently. This has become apparent in the matter of liturgy, which is a right-brain activity of great prophetic significance. Or at least it should be. It is, therefore, an area of great vulnerability in the system that seeks to keep belief and culture separate but in a strictly controlled relationship. It is often a battlefield, for that reason. Those who wish to retain control prefer the loss of meaning to the loss of control, and others fight to make liturgy a place of intercession, of grief and healing, anger and hope, of prophetic proclamation and energy. Liturgy is "too important to be left to liturgists," if by that we mean specialists who use and re-use half-understood symbols. But there are real "liturgists" who explore the ways people need and use symbols and how that works. It isn't easy, but we are at least outgrowing our tolerance for jolly tunes, and earnest songs lacking in vigor or originality, sloppy amateur dances, and felt banners and canned homilies and priests who crave attention. The roots are too deep and the shoots too tender for that kind of thing—and when the symbols die, they are hard to replace. But there is real liturgy being done in some places, on a tiny scale and occasionally on a huge one—in a living room where a group celebrates the Easter vigil with darkness and light, with the Exultet and with a blessing of each other with new water, old symbols in new ways, the Christ-vision on faces that know him only in the love of others, encountered for the first time. Or in the auditorium in Boston where 8,000 people celebrated the episcopal consecration of Barbara Harris with old and new, tears and love, formality and freedom, tradition and passion. Old symbols are stretched, used differently, rediscovered. It is painful, risking and absolutely necessary.

Awareness of all this matters; it goes on anyway but it happens faster if we understand how it happens, and in our world we need that speed if there is to be any hope. Study is not done only in universities, but universities can be, as I suggested, the places of intersection where new awareness is brought, as it were, to market.

There will be—there already is—a backlash. When people learn to use and develop language of belief in a truthful way that is responsive to the culture but not bound by it, there is great fear among the holders of power, as I suggested earlier. A better understanding of how belief systems are related to culture, and how faith (to which belief systems strive to give expression) guided by Lady Wisdom seeks renewed symbols, gives those who understand a sense of freedom and responsibility. They let go of the fear that their faith will crumble and they grow in confidence in the God who goes before them. Consequently, they are harder to intimidate and refuse to feel guilty. With the loss of those weapons, religious control is hard to exercise, and the panic grows.

The task for faith is to discern the incarnations of the Word of truth and allow them and care for them and provide spaces for them to grow. The paradox is that it seems, at this stage of literate culture, that we need to use the tools of literacy to understand the Word which underlies words, and how it still operates in human lives, seeking symbolic expression in systems of belief. But just as the prehistoric bard drew from the well of common memory the moment of mystery and story that gave ephemeral identity and continuity to the history-less people—and did it again and again, but never just the same—so we have to learn to live with belief systems that make use of common symbols, stories and names to embody the common self-awareness, never doing it exactly the same twice, yet always drawing from the same deep spring which is Wisdom's. And Wisdom is recognizable: the water she pours tastes right.

Finally, then, it seems that a task which, when described in terms of certain cultural categories seems impossibly confusing and exhausting, is really not so. We have to do the struggling, we have to use the categories we have, and stretch them and rearrange them and do peculiar things with them, because if we don't go through that process we cannot make the connection between our present predicament—caught between a sophisticated fundamentalism on the one hand, and a content-less feel-good spirituality on the other—and something so deeply rooted in the tradition that it is in touch with the reality that guides tradition in its making. But what we want to come to is the place of intersection, the point at which possibility becomes visible as actuality, while beyond the image of actuality we are aware of definitions slipping and sliding, right brain and left brain embracing and yet in tension, symbol spilling into flesh. There is a terrible simplicity about this, as terrible as the simplicity of Jesus taking bread and saying, "This is my body." These are all human enterprises plunged in ambiguity and yet, if we are content to live in ambiguity, full of warmth and hope and simple satisfaction. This is an experience of home coming, to the ancient hearth of humankind where our Lady Wisdom lights her fire, offers water for washing and sets her table for the traveller. That sense of home is perhaps the criterion by which we will know that our searching and arguing and losing and finding and grief and hope are somehow in touch with reality, that in our culture our struggles to say "I believe" are honest and shared.

I hope it will not seem flippant or trivial to suggest that anyone engaged in this strange exercise of homecoming which the University (any university) has set itself should begin by seeing the movie "Babette's Feast." Based on a short story by Isak Dinesen, and filmed in Danish, (and reading this story is not enough) this very simple story of vocation and transformation and reconciliation is possibly the most powerful theological statement to come out of our demented culture. It raises up for us questions about human choices, when both of the lovingly tyrannical minister's daughters refuse the possibility of different and richer lives in order to stay with their father; about the right use of money when Babette, the penniless refugee serving as cook in the sisters' home, spends all her 10,000 franc lottery winnings to create "Babette's feast"; about riches and poverty ("an artist is never poor"); but most of all, about the spiritual and the material, about the crushing of that distinction, about the great vocation to do just that and the discipline and effort that involves, about the love that is released and the holy foolishness it licenses, so that the "messianic banquet" ceases to be a theological in-phrase and takes on taste and smell and leaves behind dirty dishes and affirms eternal life.

This deceptively unpretentious film is the kind of thing that people of faith need to be seeing and also making, in stories, books, music,visual arts, drama, cooking, community, liturgy, farming and politics. And so on. To find salvation and to be able to believe, we have to allow the experience and the expression of life to find forms that are about home coming, that taste good. This requires honesty and care and reflection, skills and effort and patience and imagination. To return to the point at which I began, our ideal should be to experience the inadequacy of once-truthful belief systems, not as an embarrassment, or as a loss of faith, but as the dying flowers whose summer is over. It is sad, and it is also glorious to paint them and describe them and sing about them and grieve for them, so that we do not forget. But it is more important to be watching for and caring for the new flowers. And they are never exactly the same, because the old flowers have died and rotted and provided the soil from which the new ones will grow, and so that soil is not the same as it was before and the new flowers are not the same either.

Religion and the Third Sector

John A. Coleman, S.J.
Jesuit School of Theology at Berkeley

Recently, I served as an outside consultant to the Lilly Endowment concerning the first generation of grants they have distributed under a relatively new rubric: religion and the third sector. The "Third Sector" (an unfortunate and undesirable term since it serves as a mere residual cateogry) refers to the not-for-profit voluntary or independent sector. The third sector is neither profit-generating business nor government—although the activities of both have major impact on the third sector. It is not really an independent sector since nearly half of all the support received by non-profit organizations in this country is supplied by various agencies of government.[1] Nor is it well-conceived simply as a private sector since the third sector serves public purposes. Finally, the third sector is not, always and effectively, a voluntary sector of society.

The driving intuition which led the Lilly Endowment to this new area of social scientific grants derives, in part, from Alexis de Tocqueville's justly famous remark in *Democracy in America* that religion (at least in the 1840's when Tocqueville was writing) constituted the "first of America's political institutions."[2] This was so, argued Tocqueville, not because religion or any one church was politically established in America. Rather, religion and the churches play a pivotal civic role, first, by animating a vigorous voluntary sector where ideals and the embodiment of an active participatory citizenship flourish. This voluntary sector provides a crucial communal buffer between the individual and the state, protecting against the despotic tendencies of a majoritarian but atomistic democracy. The voluntary sector anchors *in institutions* and not merely *in thought*, a real distinction between the state and society crucial for a republic. Hence, the third sector is properly a *public sector* of discourse and activity about societal goals and goods uncontrolled by the state as such. The third sector functions as a public sphere—a *locus* of public discourse about the collective values of society. It provides an arena in which fundamental values, both political and non-political, can be discussed, symbolized, experimented with or ritually embodied.

Secondly, religion provides the moral habits of selfless service to the common good which undergird a republic. Religion must have an indispensable role in generating what Robert Bellah and his associates have called "habits of the heart" (i.e., moral character in the service of a common cultural ideal of the common good) which undergird a democratic form of life. Industry can not, alone, be trusted to do this since it extolls self-interest and mere utilitarian motives above service to the common good. Even if it includes the common good as a motif, the common good remains subordinate to profit as the controlling factor. Moreover, the state which would try to monopolize the inculcation of national character formation would verge on a totalitarianism.[3] Tocqueville provided the classic understanding of the public purposes of the voluntary church when he insisted that the churches serve as seed-beds for public-spirited citizenship and service to the common good.

The late 1980's, palpably, are not the early 1840's when Tocqueville wrote. In a very thoughtful overview of the current state of American religion entitled, *The Restructuring of American Religion: Society and Faith Since World War II,* Princeton sociologist of religion, Robert Wuthnow, notes a relative eclipse of the public social role of religion due to a decline in the voluntary sector.

Religious organizations have for the most part carried out their tasks in the private sector. Consequently, any significant penetration of the private sector by government represents a diminished sphere of activity in which religious groups may be able to operate. This potential for conflict between religion and the state is especially apparent if it is recalled . . . that up until the end of World War II, religious organizations played a substantial role in providing for many of the social services that government has more recently begun to appropriate for itself. By some indications, religious organizations had been responsible in the period just prior to World War II for approximately 15% of all hospitals, 42% of all homes for the aged and at least a third of all institutions of higher education . . . With the significant growth of government in all these areas since World War II, the relative role played by religion has become much less important. Not surprisingly, many have argued, religious organizations have had to develop other kinds of appeals, for example, the privatized therapeutic offerings.[4]

which have grown apace in the churches.

There can be little question about a massive and ramified state expansion since World War II into the area of welfare expenditures and of the growth of various forms of large state bureaucracies and regulatory agencies. On a theoretical level, Jürgen Habermas has described what he calls "civil privatism" as he notes how this expanding role of the state erodes voluntary participation in other secondary groups.[5] The civil or societal dimension becomes eclipsed or privatized. It becomes, then, empirically more difficult to justify a distinction between state and society.

Habermas contends that various contradictions inherent in the state in advanced societies erode membership in those organizations which link individual citizens to the public sphere and facilitate what he calls "public will formation" (and we might also call "public discourse and consensus formation"). In his work, Habermas does not focus on the churches as such. Rather, he is concerned with many kinds of political action groups (e.g., schools, community agencies and fraternal organizations) which provide spheres of "communicative action" about public values. As the state expands, argues Habermas, citizens become less involved in these kinds of voluntary associations. Robert Wuthnow and Clifford Nass have tested Habermas' theoretical point empirically. They discovered that "variation in government expenditure across states is negatively associated with voluntary membership in religious organizations . . . controlling for effects of urbanization, residential mobility, percent Catholic, percent black."[6] In other words, the larger the state budgets in the various American state governments, the lower the percentage of voluntary membership in religious organizations. Wuthnow and Nass also note that the 200,000 Protestant congregations in the United States compare favorably with only 37,000 privately-sponsored human service agencies, 14,000 national non-profit associations, 2,000 cultural organizations and 3,500 private hospitals. Religious voluntary associations form the bulk of the third sector. Their fate is tied to that of the third sector.

The consequence of civil privatism is largely negative for the maintenance of democracy. On the one hand, an atomized mass society of individuals linked together only by the mass media could be subject to propagandistic appeals or to totalitarian manipulation. Thus, Bellah and his associates look to a strengthened voluntary associational life as an indispensible brake to restrain what they term "the pull toward administrative despotism."[7]

In his discussions of civil privatism, Habermas raises questions about the capacity of a privatized world view to withstand larger cultural and societal changes. He speaks of a species of "colonization" of elements of the third sector by commercial industry and the state. Power and money have become the major "steering mechanisms" or generalized units of exchange in modern society. Not only has the voluntary sector been eclipsed relative to the profit and state sectors, but it feels new intrusive pressures from them in its own sphere, threats to any autonomous existence. It is worth noting that with demographic changes most women, even when married, now work full-time so that an earlier demographic pool of volunteers has dried up with no obvious alternative—non-sexist—pool to replace it. Perhaps, pressures could be exerted on the for-profit sector or the state to contribute volunteer time from its employees or perhaps some other arrangement to bolster volunteer recruitment could be found. But thus far it seems unlikely that "a thousand points of light" (to use George Bush's campaign slogan) will flourish, absent some larger channeling mechanism. In any event, increasingly, Americans give less money and time proportionately to the voluntary sector and we have neither the finances nor the European ethos for a government subsidy for it. Studies in philanthropy have shown how few of the really rich actually donate large sums to charities and voluntary organizations. Ironically, as Gianfranco Poggi has argued, the very social welfare programs taken over by the state from the private (frequently religious) sector may be imperilled if the state continues to attempt to reduce its costs by economizing on the welfare state in order to stimulate economic growth and expansion. Yet these cutbacks in government funds for social welfare in the 1980's, in turn, raise questions about the capacity of private non-profit organizations to fill the gap. Many of our social services (e.g., care for the homeless, hungry and unemployed, care for persons with AIDS) still depend heavily on the non-profit sector. Nevertheless, many non-profit organizations also face uncertain futures. Church colleges must withstand serious competition from tax-supported (and thus cheaper) public institutions of learning. Church-sponsored hospitals now vie with large chains of for-profit health delivery systems. Small community organizations face expanding demands for services (caring for persons with AIDS in our large cities being the key example) against inadequate donations of money and time.

A Second Intuition

A second intuition which led the Lilly Endowment to a new generation of social science grants about religion and the third sector was a recognition that theologians and church educators increasingly pay more attention to issues of church and politics (following, in this, a focus on church-state issues) or on church and the economy (with, for example, moral evaluations of for-profit capitalism and its impact on human welfare), but scant the mediating voluntary associations with whose fate the churches as voluntary associations are intimately linked and which have historically served as the main institutional bridge between church and society. Since the ground-breaking work of James Luther Adams and the early essays of James Gustafson, this focus of church-society investigation focused on the voluntary sector has been almost totally eclipsed.[8]

Thus, an internal and informal memo to us consultants from the program director of the religion and third-sector section at the Lilly Endowment notes, "Studies on voluntary organizations tend to neglect the religious factor (including the possible contributions of religious studies); religious studies tend to neglect studies of voluntary organizations (and their possible contributions)." The memo then asks, "Do any of the projects funded so far provide satisfactory explanations of this mutual neglect?" None did. Put in other terms, would a more secular civil voluntarism flourish without the motivational input and channeling of a vigorous church life which inculcates a life of service, altruism and concern for the common good? Would a more secular altruism and a service orientation decline in pervasiveness and power if the churches became eclipsed? What would happen to the voluntary church, on the other hand, if the larger, more secular, voluntary third sector diminished significantly?

It seems evident that voluntary associations with greater degrees of specialization than most religious organizations are better able to adapt to state expansion. The tremendous growth of special interest, single-purpose lobby groups in recent years attests to this greater potential. Insofar as the state has actually developed collaborative relations with some types of voluntary agencies, religious organizations may be in a relatively unfavorable position because of constitutional restrictions separating church and state.[9] Single-purpose lobby groups flourish under governmental expansion. Multi-purpose voluntary groups, such as the church, do not. Indeed, the great religious growth industry in the post-war period has been in single-purpose religious groups such as FISH (Friends in

Service Here) which provides services to the elderly and handicapped, and various specialized groups dealing in world hunger, etc. Robert Wuthnow comments, "During the 1960's and early 1970's, special-purpose groups grew at a pace at least a third faster than denominations." There is "a tendency for fewer and fewer of these special-purpose groups to be associated with denominations. Forty-seven percent of the special purpose groups that were founded prior to 1960 had clear denominational sponsorship of one kind or another. In comparison, only 32% of the groups founded since 1960 have had denominational sponsorship. Comparing the two time periods also shows that the proportion of special purpose groups that were clearly non-denominational increased from 18% to 39% of the total."[10]

The Loss of an Appropriate Third-Sector Language

Earlier I spoke of an invasion or colonization of the third sector by the state and the for-profit sector. The most telling invasion involves the loss of a language of discourse for this intermediate public sphere which is neither state nor economy. With the eclipse of public discourse appropriate to the voluntary sphere (discourse which, although about the public good, is not controlled by either state or economy), the languages of the state (with heavy emphasis on questions of legality or an interest consolidation which tends to lack any substantive vision of justice or the common good and to substitute a purely procedural notion of justice for more substantive discourse) or the language of the economy (stressing efficiency, profit generation and profit-maximizing motifs) tend to predominate, even in third sector discussion. Thus, Robert Bellah and his associates in their *Habits of the Heart* claim that our public language has become deeply impoverished by being reduced either to utilitarian (interest maximization) or therapeutic (privatized) language. While they claim that we, as a people, are better, more altruistic, than our language, they document the erosion of those "communities of memory" which would allow a different voice to be heard about the common good than mere interest aggregation and the adjudication—by balancing—of divergent and incommensurable interests.

One might argue that even the research and thinking about the third sector itself has increasingly been ruled by norms and values derived from the state and the for-profit sector. Thus, we face new questions about whether it is more efficient and cost-effective (predominant for-profit language) to run hospitals and clinics as non-profit or profit organizations. The government intrudes questions about whether social services can be more effectively administered through a single, centralized hierarchy or through greater de-centralized cooperative arrangements. Countless conferences and seminars each year focus on how non-profit organizations can enhance their appeal to certain constituencies in order to consolidate or expand their "market share," how they can compete for scarce resources against other non-profit agencies, how they can be best governed and administered or use legal loopholes to their advantage. If I can cite a personal example, I recall my utter irritation at the way the board of trustees of a Catholic college on which I served insistently spoke of the college as being competitive with other comparable educational "businesses" (the actual term used in discussions). Even in the world of philanthropy and the non-profit foundations such language predominates. Indeed, even in the churches—especially in the church-growth movement so prominent in American Protestantism—the same "bottom line" entrepreneurial discourse reigns.[11]

Does the Third Sector Really Provide Alternatives?

Probably no sector has felt this invasion or colonization more than voluntary health institutions, especially denominational hospitals. The growth in the past decades of for-profit hospitals and HMO's, on the one hand, and the increasing value of religious heterogeneity of hospital staff and clientele and increased governmental regulations, on the other hand, have put a massive squeeze on denominational hospitals such that their very institutional viability is at stake, let alone their survival and flourishing as truly alternative (e.g., more person-centered, spiritual, holistic, socially engaged in a genuine option to serve the poor, etc.) modes of health care.[12]

It is fashionable for religious schools, hospitals and charity organizations to argue, rhetorically, that as voluntary associations they serve as experimental units for new societal practices and embody alternative values not found in for-profit or state-run agencies. They plead the case for the voluntary sector as a true alternative loci of service and values. Yet scholars such as Lester Salomon, Alan Abramson and Ralph Kramer have pointed out how dependent on state funds are most voluntary associations that deliver social services.[13]

David Harrington Watt notes:

Studies of those sorts of voluntary associations demonstrate that they must almost always follow regulations drawn up by officers of the state and that they must sometimes take care to see that they do not behave in ways that offend the government. Thus it is not altogether clear that these particular agencies actually do embody values and practices that are truly alternative. Certainly, there is relatively little empirical support for the notion that bureaucrats in voluntary social service agencies necessarily behave in ways that differ dramatically from the behavior of bureaucrats in governmental agencies.

There is, on the other hand, a good deal of empirical evidence to support the claim that voluntary associations often behave in ways which conform fairly closely to models first worked out to explain the way that business corporations work. And of course there is a growing sentiment within the third sector that voluntary associations should wholeheartedly embrace entrepreneurial values and practices. Many of the leaders of voluntary associations are entirely convinced, as one recent publication put it, that 'profit-making enterprise is a legitimate and necessary way of sustaining a non-profit organization.'[14]

Few are the religious trustees in hospital or other social service settings who find the linguistic openings in the dominant agenda discussions about legality or legal complications or operating at a profit to even broach, let alone sustain, meaningful discussions of distributive justice for the poor, quality of life issues, etc. The language of the law and profit drive out competitive languages. The point, of course, is not to contend that there is some inherent evil in either the state or for-profit enterprises or that their languages are inappropriate in their own proper spheres. But when their languages predominate also in the third sector, the viability and flourishing and future of a truly alternative voluntary sector comes into jeopardy. Although, in principle, there exists no difficulty in conceiving appropriately different, if related, "spheres of justice" or in seeing the state, for-profit and the third sector as complementary rather than as engaged in a zero-sum competitive game, in practice the first two sectors seem to have "colonized the life-World" appropriate to the third sector. This is an issue for religion.

The Lilly Endowment's internal memo to us consultants asked: "To what extent is the very idea of a third sector dependent on skepticism about people's ability to reach a reasoned consensus on any sufficiently substantial notion of the common good? Would such skepticism necessarily reduce people's ideas of the common good to private, arbitrary preferences? Or can 'reasoned consensus' be given a more pluralistic interpretation?"

In addressing these questions, we consultants preferred to refer to the third sector as a public sphere—as much public as private—a locus of public discourse about the collective values of the society, an arena in which fundamental values can be discussed, experimented with and symbolized, where public debate is nurtured. We saw it, in Habermas' terms, as the most appropriate area in a democracy for "public will formation" and "public discourse in forming a societal consensus."[15] Clearly, something such as this notion of the third sector lay behind the American bishops' two ground-breaking pastorals on peace and the economy. The bishops were as concerned with "public will formation" and discourse about the common good as in the substantive text of their documents.

Some Signs of Hope

Perhaps, however, there is hope for a renewed attention to the issues raised when religion is viewed in respect to the third sector. There are new developments worth noting:

(1) Courses for undergraduates on the role of philanthropy in American life are developing where, surely, the pivotal role of religious philanthropy as the largest source of charitable giving in America will merit discussion. The Association of American Colleges has been awarding $15,000 a year to 16 colleges to develop model courses on philanthropy in American life. These grants have also been underwritten by the W.K. Kellogg Foundation and other donors.

(2) Presently, 19 colleges and universities operate centers on philanthropy and non-profit organizations. Only one such center existed a decade ago. Half of these centers have been created since 1986 alone.

(3) Foundation interest in the study of philanthropy and non-profit organizations grows. The Lilly Endowment foresees awards of more than $8 million in grants for teaching, research and public service projects connected with this topic. The Ford and W. K. Kellogg Foundations and the Rockefeller Brothers' Fund have each made grants of more than $1 million for similar research.

(4) Case Western Reserve University recently received a major gift of $2.5 million for a center on non-profit organizations, and New York University received a donation of $2.8 million for a center on philanthropy and law.

(5) Several universities now offer specializations on the management of non-profit organizations leading to the M.A. degree.

(6) Two academic publishers, Jossey Bass and Transaction Books, have begun a new series of books on philanthropy and non-profit organizations. Indiana University and Jossey Bass have also announced plans to publish journals explicitly devoted to the non-profit sector in American society.

One theoretical thread in all this new activity is a conviction that philanthropy is a social instrument which helps to compensate for the shortcomings of the marketplace and the state. It is seen as a public and social good. John C. Simon, co-chair of Yale University's pioneering program on non-profit organizations comments: "We need to make available to students the values of a life of service in the public interest, just as we would the qualities of fine music or political freedom."

Despite these new initiatives, some fear that a new focus on the third sector could evaporate when the grant support from foundations ends. They doubt the commitment of the universities and colleges to continue this work. Other fears point to the possibility that the new schools and departments might degenerate into mere vocational credentialling units for certifying members for the fundraising profession. In any event, a recent article in *The Chronicle of Higher Education*, treating of this renewed academic interest in the third sector, laments that most academics remain "pathetically uninformed about the subject's importance in American life."[16]

Five Restructurings of American Religion

I want now to draw upon Robert Wuthnow's analysis in his *The Restructuring of American Religion* to suggest five important changes in religion and culture in the United States since World War II, and then highlight their impact on the question of religion and the third sector. According to Wuthnow, these major shifts or restructurings of American religion since World War II have been:

(1) *The Declining Significance of Denominationalism*

An earlier period of American society saw denominationalism (or, at least, Will Herberg's famous tri-partite Protestant/Catholic/ Jew) as a significant focus of identity, commitment and loyalty.[17] Religion played a quasi-ethnic role in society. Membership in a denomination tended to carry with it ramifying and overlapping loyalties to kin, friendship and even job-related attachments. But, perhaps as H. Richard Niebuhr argued 60 years ago, much of American distinctive denominationalism was rooted as much in social as theological factors.[18] As those social factors changed, so would the distinctive pattern of America as a denominational society. With time (and an ecumenical movement which since Vatican II embraces Catholics as well as Protestants), the classic inter-denominational cleavages and deep conflicts have diminished. At any rate, inter-faith and inter-denominational hostility in America has dramatically declined.[19]

Church-switching across denominations has risen from a mere 4% of the population in the 1950's to nearly 33% in the 1980's. Neither Judaism nor Catholicism has been entirely spared this erosion of denominational identity. Inter-marriage rates across denominations have also soared. Members of one denomination now tend to have very positive and "friendly" attitudes towards members of other religious groups (this was certainly not true in the early 1950's when inter-religious conflict was salient). In an earlier period, denominational loyalties were deeply rooted and sharply defined. We note, for example, the still major salience of denominational loyalties and identities in the Lynd's famous Middletown studies of the 1930's.[20] As late as the 1960's, Charles Glock and Rodney Stark could still find that people drew most of their closest friends from their own denomination.[21] But as Wuthnow comments about the 1980's, "High rates of denominational switching and interdenominational marriage, reduced levels of denominational identity and cross-denominational tensions, as well as pervasive amounts of contact across denominational lines (4 in 5 Americans have attended a religious service other than one of their own denomination)—all point toward a declining monopoly of specific religious traditions over the enactment of religious conviction."[22] Belief and belonging (the two major vectors of religious commitment) no longer strongly correlate. People believe what they choose but still belong to churches.

One consequence of the loss of denominational identity is a reinforcement of religious individualism or religious privatism which plays into the "civil privatism" of Habermas. The overwhelming majority of the population holds to strongly individualistic views of religion. In a Gallup poll, a staggering 81% agreed with the statement, "An individual should arrive at his or her own religious beliefs independent of any churches or synagogues." Seventy percent of churchgoers say that one can be a good Christian or Jew without attending church or synagogue.[23] In matters of belief and morality, the individual is her or his own final arbiter. In a society where religion is a voluntary activity, the successful inculcation of the sort of habits of the heart Tocqueville talked about depends on the churches being able to maintain a strong sense of inner discipline and commitment. This, too, becomes increasingly hard for them to do. Even Catholics, in larger numbers, adhere to a kind of selective or "pick and choose" Catholicism.

In an important survey, *Religious Change in America*, Andrew Greeley contests the claims for a decline of denominationalism in America. He avers, "America is still a denominational society. The best 'fit' for the data is a model which indicates stability of affiliation with the identity Protestant, Catholic or Jew. In short, denominationalism has not changed much, *although patterns of denominational affiliation have altered dramatically*."[24] The italicized phrase points to the growth in conservative evangelical churches and an increase of switching toward them from the mainline liberal Protestant churches. Yet Greeley restricts his analysis to individual religiosity, neglects to test salience and depth of denominational loyalties, leaves unanalyzed the reduction in inter-denominational hostility and the evisceration of overlapping and reinforcing loyalties attached to denominational loyalty. To be sure, Greeley is right to assert that American Catholics, Jews and Protestants do not, in large numbers, switch across these divides (although Protestant switching increases within its family pool). But even Greeley must concede, "patterns of denominational affiliation have altered dramatically."

On one other point, Greeley is absolutely correct. Notoriously, Americans are not secularist. Overwhelming numbers of Americans pray, believe in God and life after death, accept the bible as God's word, adhere to the divinity of Christ. But as Wade Roof and William McKinney state in their excellent survey of contemporary American religion, *American Mainline Religion*, "One could say that the enemy of church life in this country is not so much secularity as it is do-it-yourself religiosity."[25] Do-it-yourself religiosity feeds into civil privatism and erodes the distinctiveness of the third sector as an arena of substantive commitments and debates about the public good.

(2) *The Proliferation of Special-Purpose Religious Groups*

As already mentioned, special-purpose religious lobby or service groups have grown phenomenally since World War II—most of them special-purpose groups free of explicit denominational sponsorship. Of the 800 special-purpose religious groups recognized by the IRS as religious voluntary groups, few are church or denomination-based. Most, such as *Bread for the World* and *Habitat for Humanity* or anti-abortion groups, are interdenominational. Wuthnow makes an important point when he reminds us that the 7% of Americans who claim involvement in religious hunger ministries are comparable to the percent of the general public which lists membership in the nation's largest Protestant denomination (Southern Baptists). The 5% which claims involvement in positive-thinking seminars equals the size of the nation's second-largest Protestant denomination (Methodists). Even the 2-3% who claim involvement in religiously-motivated anti-nuclear or holistic health movements are larger than most denominations.[26] Other religious groupings besides denominations have entered the religious map of

America. Denominations, frequently, become a kind of holding-company for an increasing number of special interest groups, e.g., Catholic Golden Age Members, the Fellowship of Christian Athletes, gay, women's, ecological and anti-nuclear caucuses. While such special-purpose, single-issue religious lobbies represent a species of voluntarism, the unique focus on a single issue further fragments the body politic rather than providing an alternative third-sector arena for substantive public discourse about the common good.

(3) *From Consensus to a Liberal-Conservative Divide*

American religion has restructured from the consensus views of the 1950's into a liberal-conservative divide (but note, *within* as much as across denominations), with each position of relatively equal strength (43% more liberal; 41% more conservative). Each links up with different versions of our civil religion (more prophetic vs. more defensive patriotisms), holding alternative myths and visions and stories about the meaning of America. Each views the other with distinctively skeptical attitudes and holds very negative stereotypes of the other. The new denominationalism, as noted, is not between but within denominations such that some conservative Catholics look closer to conservative evangelicals than to their fellow, but progressive, Catholics. Even American evangelicalism is much more divided than a stereotypical view might allow.[27] This new denominationalism makes a church consensus on a culture-affirming or contra-cultural stance more difficult to achieve, with the result that the churches themselves, like the larger political order, frequently extoll a pluralism without content. Again, this new denominationalism feeds into civil privatism.

(4) *The Growth of Alternative Sources of Values*

Religion must now vie with a triad of "secular" values (individual freedom, material success and the wonders and myth of technology) as competing legitimacy systems. Even opponents of these three deeply-rooted and reinforcing cultural motifs are seduced into appealing to these three themes to gain a wider cultural hearing.[28]

Of the value of individual freedom, Richard J. Neuhaus has said, "Much of the course of public reasoning in America can be read from the fact that our highest appeals are no longer to Providence but to privacy."[29] Of the technological myth, sociologist Robert Nisbet claims, "Technology, for many Americans, is not simply a good thing: it is in its own way millennialist, offering a happiness beyond earlier dreams to the world, and with America leading the way."[30] Notoriously, technology deals with means, not ends. It is blind to substantive goods as such. Nevertheless, some choices for technological advance (e.g., a choice for nuclear energy) preclude and entirely foreclose more decentralized "appropriate" technology.

Unfortunately, argues Wuthnow, American faith in technology is virtually immune to the criticism or doubts that might arise from the risks (e.g., radiation pollution or environmental damage) accompanying the growth of technology. Thus, "Mythologization of technology comes at the point when a full range of public values cannot be seriously debated because technical considerations have already ruled some of them out."[31] Wuthnow also deplores the craving for a quick technological fix.

> In a subtle, but perhaps important, way, technology has, therefore, become linked with that most fundamental value—freedom—on which Americans rely to legitimate their way of life. If the marketplace gradually redefined freedom to mean freedom of choice, technology now begins to replace the marketplace as the main source of that kind of freedom. Not simply the modern supermarket with its panoply of choices but The Electronic Candy Store filled with word processors and software becomes the symbol of our expanded freedom to choose.[32]

But we should make no mistake about it. The three values of individual freedom, material success and the wonders of technology form the very skeletal body of American culture. While they can undermine traditional religious norms and values, their myths are so deeply rooted in the American psyche that the churches must incorporate their motifs to gain a cultural hearing. None of these three reinforce a tradition or community of memory so necessary if the third sector would provide an alternative language to power and money, to supplement them, not supplant them entirely, as the prime steering mechanisms of our society.

(5) *The Expansion of the State*

The last restructuring of American religion involves the growing role of the state in organizing modern society. State expansion raises anew the increasingly problematic symbolic boundaries between church and state such that older, seemingly settled, *formulae* for adjudicating church-state disputes no longer hold. Thus, we face new questions such as, "Does the IRS have the power to determine what constitutes a religious activity? Can they rule out social justice ministries as being more political than religious? Can the state avoid involvement in abortion or gender issues?" The classic American case for the public church assumed a separation of church and state which did not entail a separation of church and society as such. The voluntary church, through para-denominational social movements and voluntary associations, in the arena of the third sector, brought to bear public debate and discourse about the directions of the society. With the expansion of the state, church-society relations now touch more often sensitive church-state issues.

The memo of the Lilly Endowment for us consultants on religion and the third sector asked us to consider the following questions: "Religion and the third sector is one of the two areas of study funded by the Lilly Endowment which aim to understand various 'streams' of religious life in their wider cultural or social setting. The other area is labeled 'church and society'. What are the advantages of keeping these two areas distinct? What are the disadvantages?"

Conceptually distinguishing church and state from church and third sector remains advantageous in order to save the important distinction between state and society. There is a legitimate social arena which is neither business nor government. Yet the boundaries among the three sectors are neither fully distinct nor impermeable. The line between the state and the third sector remains as vague and shifting as the line between the third sector and the market. For that matter, the line between the state and the market is also vague and fluctuating in modern economies. The market neither is nor can be as "free" of government regulation or subsidy as the absolute ideologists of a free market would desire. Most often, such ideologists want government support, sustenance and indirect subsidy for the market without any of its regulation! Clearly, however, various kinds of resources pass across the three sectors. For example, the third sector can receive legitimacy and sustenance from the state (with, for example, state subsidies being subcontracted to the voluntary sector). Indeed, some kinds of governmental policies can actually entice into existence a proliferation of new voluntary activities and groups. In its turn, the third sector can contribute ideas about collective directions or serve as an experimental laboratory for new processes which the state would then later take over for implementation and generalization to the society at large. The third sector receives financial contributions from the marketplace and adopts entrepreneurial organizational models. In return, the third sector provides essential *social* services (e.g., care for the unemployed, the homeless, the hungry) which alleviate the social strains and pressures and dislocations flowing from a market economy. Moreover, in comparative studies of different societies—or of the same society at different time frames—we find that the third sector may constitute at one time a larger share of the whole and in other cases and times a smaller share of the whole.[33]

The renewed academic concern with questions of religion and the third sector assumes that state expansion and the incursion of the market into areas hitherto reserved to the third sector (e.g., health care, some social services for profit) have reduced the third sector's share of the whole. It further assumes that the declining share of the third sector raises crucial questions and challenges to the public role of the church and to the public will-formation and societal discourse. State expansion, especially, jeopardizes the critical distinction between state and society on which democracy rests. Hence, attempts to retrieve the church-society nexus by reinvigorating the third sector will necessarily unsettle earlier partial compromises on church-state issues.

Research Themes Connected with Religion and the Third Sector

At the formal conference inaugurating the Jesuit Institute at Boston College, each of the presenters was asked to suggest directions for research and study at the Institute based on our substantive remarks. I suggest three such areas not only for the Institute but, more generally, for denominational colleges and universities in the United States concerned with the vital nexus between belief and culture.

(1) I have been arguing that this whole issue of a public sphere (the third sector), which is neither exclusively government nor the economy, and the discovery of an appropriate language of public discourse about a substantive common good, which is neither purely self-interest or therapy language or the language of the aggregation of divergent interests, is crucial for the very future of the public church. Indeed, I take it that this is *the most pressing arena* of the religion-society nexus in our day. On its fate, to some extent, depends the continuation of a Catholic construal (as opposed to a pure witness ethic) of church and society in a pluralistic modern political environment. Catholic theories of church and society have always built in some version, however attenuated, of natural law and the cooperative engagement of Catholics with fellow citizens in a *common* endeavor. They have never been content only with witnessing from their particularist and revelational warrants. The Jesuit Institute at Boston College and denominational colleges, more

generally, need to be in the forefront of the study and research on the third sector's public and social role. Put bluntly, the continuing public mission of the church stands or falls on the continuing viability and flourishing of the third sector in American society. The voluntary church in America (and there are simply no other kinds of churches in America) relies on a wider climate (cultural and institutional) of sustenance of the third sector.

(2) A question posed to the Lilly Endowment consultants on religion and the third sector reads as follows: "The critical pursuit of knowledge seems to require 'relative freedom from political constraints and market pressures.' Yet it often seems to flourish most in state-supported (first sector) schools, where academic freedom can be invoked almost automatically. Private (third sector) schools are often free to purge their faculties for raising unwelcome questions, though some acknowledge academic freedom of some sort as a moral obligation apart from legal consequences. To what extent is the critical pursuit of knowledge a third-sector matter? Is it safe to assume, as these reflections do, that some sort of academic freedom is required for the critical pursuit of knowledge to flourish?"

The issue of pluralism in American society and the role of the Catholic university within it remains an unresolved issue in American Catholic life. On the one hand, the Charles Curran affair at the Catholic University of America and the cross-cultural conflicts between the Vatican and the American Catholic academic community underscore the importance of the issue. On the other hand, some Catholic academics (I think mindlessly) talk about academic freedom by invoking a purely secular notion of academic freedom whose crucial assumption remains agnosticism about ever achieving anything like the truth, an assumption clearly at variance with Catholic belief in revelation. In many of the procedures of the regnant secular notion of academic freedom, one may find much to adopt for Catholic universities. But the agnostic assumption of this secular model cannot be accepted. Nevertheless, absent any real and thoughtful Catholic theory and foundation (with appropriate procedures) of academic freedom, most academics naturally fall back on the secular version. Others would turn the Catholic university into a mere school of catechetics, repeating what official teachers say.

A Catholic university serves not only the academic goals of research but, also, equally, the church and society. Thus, just as we needed at Vatican Council II to discover a uniquely and appropriately *Catholic* rationale for religious freedom which did not buy into religious indifferentism (the complaint of the Vatican to secular foundations for religious freedom), so we will need to find a distinctively *Catholic* underpinning for academic freedom in the Catholic university. Like the Catholic case for religious liberty (which eschewed the religious agnosticism of secular versions), a Catholic rationale for academic freedom will be analogous (both similar and different) to regnant secular agnostic theories of academic freedom. Quite clearly, the Catholic community is not, at present, in possession of a theory of academic freedom that is both appropriately Catholic and appropriate to a university as such.

Many of the discussions about Catholic universities have focused rather exclusively either on this issue of an appropriate Catholic academic freedom in the university, or have sought ways to make the university a kind of moral community which shores up the church as community and leads to "discipline" in the older religious sense of a community of discipline based on shared prayer, belonging, belief and behavior. But I would like here to focus on a slightly different approach to the question. Notoriously, American universities reflect the non-substantive pluralism of American society. Put bluntly, they know how to pursue knowledge, to share and converse about it, and propagate it, but they do not know how to answer the still-telling question of Robert Lynd in the 1930's: "Knowledge for what, serving what societal ends and goals?"[34]

If the university—which by its name connotes a kind of healthy pluralism—cannot really find a free way, short of authoritarian intrusions, to answer these questions, it will not well serve either church or society. A telling alternative to the techno-rational multi-university presupposes a telling critique of society and culture. This would be difficult to achieve in a university in the best of circumstances. Can we achieve it with a constituency of students, faculty, administrators who are not Catholic or even Christian (as increasingly the constituency of many Catholic colleges are not)? It will not do to simply keep invoking the *rhetoric* of "a Catholic university." A university conspiracy to find common purpose and substantive goals in the university becomes, in microcosm, a mirror of the task of our whole society.

If the Catholic university—a segment of the third sector which joins church and society, religion and culture—cannot become a free arena of public debate and discourse about the substantive goods of society, probably the church, as such, cannot achieve this in the wider society. The classic American Catholic church-society strategy in a voluntary society may rise or fall on the freedom of its universities to undertake this task of a "pluralistic conspiracy to achieve a common good." Freedom of discourse undictated by state or market is the hallmark of the third sector, as it is of the university. I want to argue that construing a new rationale for academic freedom in a Catholic setting demands not only attention to the Catholic university's service to the church or its service to the academic world but also its role of service in society. I think if we construed the case for academic freedom in the Catholic university by connecting it to the church's wider church-society strategy in a pluralistic voluntary society in and through the third sector, we might achieve some new light on the subject. In any event, I agree fully with the Lilly Endowment memo's assumption "that some sort of genuine academic freedom is required for the critical pursuit of knowledge to flourish" and that such critical pursuit of knowledge belongs most properly in the third sector. The church's failure to articulate a credible, if fully Catholic, theory of academic freedom in its universities compromises its credibility to play a role in keeping the third sector alive. Nor is this some luxury for a Catholicism which takes seriously the Catholic doctrine of subsidiarity which, in

202 In All Things

germ, contains the Catholic case for the importance of the third sector for society.

(3) I have alluded to the triad of individual freedom, the technological paradigm and material success as the skeleton of American culture which—I have argued elsewhere—will not be exorcized by mere moralistic evocations of their opposites. All three of these cultural ideals need to be probed as American-to-the-core and tested as to the respects in which they are either inimical to or susceptible to Catholic understandings. All three need to be seen as deeply intertwined and reinforcing cultural ideals, deeply rooted in American mythic structures. Technology, in particular, its promise, deformations and the possible recovery of the original promise of technology strike me as suitable thematic topics for the Jesuit Institute at Boston College, dedicated to interdisciplinary dialogue about American culture and belief, to pursue. Once again, a key issue will involve the ability of the third sector to find a distinctive voice and platform of public discourse to address value issues about technology which the language of the state and the market cannot raise. Trying to raise them in a responsible way may uncover just how much in jeopardy the third sector is in current American society.[35]

Notes

1. Cf. Ralph M. Kramer, "The Future of the Voluntary Agency in a Mixed Economy," *Journal of Applied Behavioral Studies* 21 (1985) 377-91.

2. Alexis de Tocqueville, *Democracy in America*, edited by J. P. Mayer and Max Lerner (New York: Harper & Row, 1966).

3. Robert Bellah et al., *Habits of the Heart* (Berkeley: University of California Press, 1985). For a thoughtful reevaluation of the meaning of the common good, cf. David Hollenbach, S.J., "The Common Good Revisited," *Theological Studies* 50 (1989) 70-95.

4. Robert Wuthnow, *The Restructuring of American Religion* (Princeton, New Jersey: Princeton University Press, 1988).

5. Jürgen Habermas, *The Structural Transformation of the Public Sphere* (Cambridge, Mass.: MIT Press, 1989).

6. Robert Wuthnow and Clifford Nass, "Government Activity and Civil Privatism: Evidence from Voluntary Church Membership," *Journal for the Scientific Study of Religion* 27 (1988) 170.

7. Bellah, *Habits of the Heart* 211.

8. Cf. James Luther Adams, "Freedom and Association" in his *On Being Human Religiously* (Boston: Beacon Press, 1976) 57-89 and James Gustafson, *Treasure in Earthen Vessels* (New York: Harper & Row, 1963). For a recent theological address to the church-state issue, cf. Richard McBrien, *Caesar's Coin* (New York: MacMillan, 1987) and for church and economics, cf. Charles Strain, ed., *Prophetic Visions and Economic Realities* (Grand Rapids, Michigan: Wm. Eerdmans, 1989).

9. Robert Wuthnow and Clifford Nass, "Government Activity and Civil Privatism" 71.

10 Wuthnow, *The Restructuring of American Religion* 113.

11. For the church growth movement in Protestantism, cf. Dean Hoge and David Rozen, *Understanding Church Growth and Decline* (New York: The Pilgrim Press, 1979).

12. For pressures on Catholic hospital systems, cf. Jeanne Katherine de Blois, "The Catholic Hospital: An Analysis and Critique of the Theological Rationale for its Identity and Continued Existence." (Unpublished Ph.D. dissertation, Department of Religious Studies, The Catholic University of America, 1987).

13. Alan J. Abramson and Lester M. Salmon, *The Non-Profit Sector and the New Federal Budget* (Washington, D.C.: Urban Institute

Press, 1986) and Ralph M. Kramer, "The Future of the Voluntary Agency."

14. David Harrington Watt, unpublished mss., "The Study of Religion and the Third Sector of American Society: Theoretical Considerations," 1988.

15. I have found helpful the remarks of Robert Wuthnow in his unpublished paper, "Religion and the Third Sector," 1988.

16. Cf. Anne Lowrey Bailey, "More Scholars, Colleges Taking an Interest in the Study of Philanthropy and Non-Profit Organizations," in *The Chronicle of Higher Education* (Sept 21, 1988) 34-36. The Simon citation derives from this source.

17. Will Herberg, *Protestant, Catholic, Jew* (Garden City, New York: Doubleday Anchor Books, 1960).

18. H. Richard Niebuhr, *The Social Sources of Denominationalism* (New York: Henry Holt and Company, 1929).

19. For an earlier period of intense interreligious hostility, cf. Robert Bellah and Frederick Greenspahn, eds., *Uncivil Religion: Interreligious Hostility in America* (New York: Crossroad Publishing, 1987).

20. For the changes in Middletown since the Lynd's 1930 study, cf. Richard Fox, "Epitaph for Middletown" in Richard Fox and Jackson Lears, eds., *The Culture of Consumption* (New York: Basic Books, 1983).

21. Charles Glock and Rodney Stark, *American Piety* (Berkeley: University of California Press, 1967).

22. For the evidence for the decline of denominationalism in America, cf. Wuthnow, *The Restructuring of American Religion* 88-99.

23. Cited in Wade Roof and William McKinney, *American Mainline Religion* (New Brunswick: Rutgers University Press, 1987) 56.

24. Andrew Greeley, *Religious Change in America* (Cambridge, Mass.: Harvard University Press, 1989).

25. Roof and McKinney, *American Mainline Religion* 56.

26. Wuthnow, *The Restructuring of American Religion* 120.

27. For a judicious view of the divisions in American evangelicalism, cf. James Davidson Hunter, *Evangelicalism: Conservative Religion and the Quandary of Modernity* (New Brunswick: Rutgers University Press, 1983) and *Evangelicalism: The Coming Generation* (Chicago: University of Chicago Press, 1987).

28. I treat of these three themes of freedom, technology and material success as deeply-rooted American cultural myths at greater length in my "American Culture as a Challenge to Catholic Intellectuals" in Cassian Veuhaus, ed., *American Culture and Catholicism* (Mahwah, New Jersey: Paulist Press, 1990).

29. Cited in Wuthnow, *The Restructuring of American Religion* 282.

30. Robert Nisbet, "Utopia's Mores: Has the American Vision Dimmed?" *Public Opinion* (April/May, 1983) 9.

31. Wuthnow, *The Restructuring of American Religion* 290.

32. *Ibid.,* 293.

33. I have been informed in my remarks here by Wuthnow's unpublished 1988 mss., "Religion and the Third Sector."

34. Robert S. Lynd, *Knowledge for What?* (New York: Columbia University Press, 1939). I treat of the role of centers of learning as embodying an advocacy role *vis-a-vis* the wider society in "Objectivity and Advocacy," *Theological Education* 25, no. 2 (1989) 60-79.

35. For an excellent treatment of technology and values, cf. Albert Borgmann, *Technology and the Character of Everyday Life* (Chicago: University of Chicago Press, 1984).

"Research across the Disciplines": Four Problematic Areas for Inquiry

Michael J. Buckley, S.J.
University of Notre Dame

The goal of these presentations, as I understand it, is to explore the challenges and opportunities opened up by the new institute. This institute itself is described as a "research institute founded jointly by the Jesuit Community and the University [and] designed to help strengthen the Catholic and Jesuit character of Boston College by supporting research across the disciplines of the University." It is interesting and important that "research across the disciplines" is to strengthen the Catholic and Jesuit character. When one speaks of research, one speaks of problematic areas gradually prepared for careful inquiry through the formulation of precise questions and appropriate methods. I should like in these remarks to suggest four such areas that could well concern such an institute. An extended definition of any one of them could alone occupy this single lecture. Hence, I should like simply to describe these problematic areas briefly and schematically, drawing upon previous writings of mine in which a fuller treatment of each of them can be found.

It seems to me remarkably appropriate that the general theme under which we speak this afternoon has been set as "culture and belief." That is precisely the way that both John Dewey and Sigmund Freud framed the religious problem today.[1] If, for contrast and comparison, one looks back at major studies in the seventeenth and eighteenth centuries that attempted to establish the existence and reality of God, one will find that they build upon something quite different, upon something that confronted the knowing subject either as ideas (as in Descartes and Malebranche) or far more influentially as the physical universe (as in Newton, Samuel Clarke, and the majority of Christian apologists in the 18th century). Eventually, natural philosophy or physics won the day, becoming among many of the educated and enlightened the foundation for religious belief. When a self-confessed atheism arose in the circle of Baron d'Holbach and Denis Diderot during the Enlightenment, the grounds for its assertion were also physics. One combined the universality of Newtonian mechanics with the Cartesian assertion that mechanics must have mechanical principles. One met this second requirement by positing as a comprehensive principle a dynamic matter, whose gradual self-development could account for the design as well as for the evil in the universe.

When Laplace and Legrange insisted that there was no need to introduce the question of God into physics, a profound and pervasive Kantian influence generalized this strategy into a necessity, insisting that theoretic knowledge could not, without contradiction, entertain this issue. The question about God belonged in the ethical area, a necessary postulate of human ethical reflection if it were not to be finally absurd. It was not, nature that would justify the existence of God; it was human nature—whether that human nature was disclosed in the experience of absolute dependence, as in Schleiermacher, or transfigured dialectically in the freedom and concept of spirit, as in Hegel. Atheism followed suit. However differently Feuerbach and Marx, Schopenhauer and Nietzsche would argue, they agreed in this: that the major counter against God was the recognition of the alienation or frustration of human nature, the inhibiting of human potentiality, which belief in God worked upon human beings.

In the twentieth century, maintained both Dewey and Freud, there is a further decisive shift. The contexts for discussion become one of culture. Freud equated civilization and culture and located religious beliefs—illusions—as one of the four mental assets of a culture. Religious beliefs were fostered by human culture as a way of both reconciling human beings to the instinctual renunciations that it demanded and consoling them before the menace of nature, the terrors of life, and the prospect of death. John Dewey, possibly the most symptomatic American thinker in the twentieth century, redefined experience as the human interaction with the environment and made culture the result of this interaction. For both, this was true: Just as culture had originated the affirmation of the reality of God, so the growth of culture into increasing education, sophistication or refinement would inevitably—by what Dewey called "the method of disposal"—render the affirmation of God or religious beliefs otiose. "The growth of knowledge and of its methods has been such as to make acceptance of these [religious] beliefs increasingly onerous and even impossible for a large number of cultivated men and women."[2]

Three recent studies have indicated how very correct Dewey was. The Carnegie Study done by Lipset and Ladd, *The Divided Academy* (1975), came to a reading of the American universities and religious belief similar to previous studies of Leuba in the 20's and 30's, namely that "the more distinguished [university] faculty, were much more irreligious than their less eminent colleagues."[3] Stanley Rothman, Robert Lichter and Linda Lichter in a study still to be published, *Elites in Conflict*, have claimed parallel findings in their study of elite groups in journalism and media. The *Connecticut Mutual Life Report on American Values in the 80's: The Impact of Belief* concluded: "Those with lower, rather than higher, levels of education are more likely to be highly religious."[4] There seems to be no question that John Dewey was accurate in his assessment of culture and belief in the United States. It is a mark of our culture that the highest proportion of the religiously-alienated is found not among the urban proletariat nor the immigrants nor the workers, but among the educated elite. The causes in the culture that have led to this alienation might bear serious study. If, as Bernard Lonergan has maintained, theology is to mediate between religion and culture, does this present situation not indicate a serious weakness, even isolation, from the culture within contemporary Catholic theology in the United States? The question must be posed here—not about the effectiveness of apologetics or religious movements, but about the quality and intellectual cogency of our theological reflection and the depth of its American inculturation.

It is obvious how coordinate such a study would be to a Jesuit heritage. Many of the better moments in the history of the Society of Jesus have pointed to a profound concern for culture—both in its general sense as civilization and in its more restricted sense of human refinement and development: the care for the intellectual culture embodied in mathematics and the new sciences, the inculturation shown in the Chinese and Malabar rites, the establishment of the reductions of Paraguay, the fostering of Baroque in architecture and music, and the dedication to humanistic education. The study of contemporary American culture and its relationship to the possibilities of belief stands well within this tradition and it is an issue crucial to the Church.

This leads naturally into the second problematic area I wish to mention, that of the Catholic university in the United States. There are many elements here that remain unresolved, not to say incoherent, not only because of the history of its own growth and current pressures but also because of its unique finality. From *Gravissimum Educationis*, I take the Catholic university to be that institution of higher learning in and through which the Church "strives to relate all of human culture to the gospel of salvation."[5] That means "all" human culture: scientific, humanistic, and religious, with all of the diversity of faculty and subjects, with all of the academic freedom, that allows these to flourish authentically in the responsible growth of knowledge. "As to the range of University teaching," wrote Newman, "certainly the very name of University is inconsistent with restriction of any kind."[6]

Now it seems to me self-evident that the vitality of a university lies with the quality of inquiry on its campus. I use "inquiry" here in its widest and most generous sense: some serious and disciplined engagement with questions. If one would judge the life of a university, one should look to what originates the continual conversations, the arguments, the collaborative study, the scholarly contributions, the private research, even the serious divisions. It seems to me further evident that the character of a university will lie in the questions to which it gives priority and to the knowledge, sensibilities and skills it thinks most worth pursuing. The difference in character between Boston College and MIT, for example, is not that one has free discourse and the other does not. Free discourse is an essential for any university. The difference lies with the kind of questions that are given priority and the kind of knowledge that is judged most worth having. The Catholic character of Boston College precisely as a university does not lie in its campus ministry or its social influence or the vitality of its liturgy. All of these should be present for the general Christian life of the school, as their analogues must be present in other and very different institutions. What makes for the Catholic character of a university as a university, however, is the kind of questions to which it gives priority.

If this is true, then those who awaken these questions within a university nurture its vitality and stamp its character. I see the institute that you are projecting in this light and, indeed, with this Socratic function. To formulate real questions, as both Aristotle and Dewey insist, is itself a serious task of inquiry. It means to confront the obstacles to knowledge, the unknown, the incoherent, the ambiguous, the unsettled and to attempt to formulate a question apt enough to allow for research and inquiry. "To find out what the problem and problems are which a problematic situation presents to be inquired into," wrote John Dewey, "is to be well along in inquiry. To mistake the problem involved is to cause subsequent inquiry to be irrelevant or to go astray."[7] The shape of the problem will structure all subsequent procedures. To establish an institute whose function is such a sensitive contact with the contemporary situation that its collaborative efforts can recognize the problems that should focus the Catholic nature of the university is to make an enormous contribution to that university. What are the defining problems of a vital Catholic university today? If such problems are not to be artificially imposed upon a situation but to grow out of it, they require the collaborative interchange of many disciplines. That is why an interdisciplinary institute seems to be appropriate: a number of people collaborating from various disciplines to determine the nature of the problems with which our situation confronts the reflective intellect. I see this as the second problematic area which lies before this institute.

This, in turn, leads into the third problematic area which Catholic universities must face: the realization of theology as an architectonic discipline. Simply teaching Catholic theology on this campus does not make the university Catholic; it makes it more of a university. A university becomes Catholic when theology becomes an integrating discipline drawing the other disciplines and sciences into conversations and collective inquiry. Theology becomes architectonic to the degree that it occasions, fosters, serves, and develops this integration of these fields of disciplined reflection. Notice: I am speaking of theology, not necessarily the theology department.

When Ignatius, in the fourth part of the *Constitutions*, elaborated the form of the Jesuit university for his time, he structured one in which the justification for the liberal arts, sciences and philosophy lay with their relationship to theology.[8] Humane letters were important both to learn theology and to engage in theology.[9] Further, philosophy and science dispose the human intellect for theological studies, are useful for the complete understanding of theology, and "also by their own nature contribute to the same end."[10] In other words, Ignatius saw all of these disciplines contributing to and integrated within what was theological wisdom. Theology functioned as a unifying, architectonic study by being in vital contact with all the forms of reflective knowledge of his time. Indeed, Ignatius seems to have increasingly realized that theology, to be well done, must be a university discipline. Certainly, there is not any need to apologize for the theologians, the mathematicians and scientists, the humanists and artists that emerged from these institutions.

Our century will not repeat the structures of the sixteenth and seventeenth centuries. But there is a vision here which Jesuit universities might well attempt to retrieve now in a very different way. Our times and our institutions are vastly different, but the understanding of a theology necessarily in vital interchange with the range of human arts and sciences, of whatever passes for disciplined reflection—one might well ask how this could be achieved today, this integration of the sciences and the arts within a theological wisdom. It may well be that the integration proper to our own times will be through topics and concerns of mutual interest and of common inquiry, that theology must assume a more heuristic, a more Socratic, a more questioning stance with the other disciplines and they with it. How to foster this interrelationship of theology with the other disciplines might well engage the institute as a problematic area obviously touching both culture and belief.

Let me add a fourth problematic area.[11] Traditionally, the Jesuit university has been concerned with the humanities, and Ignatius' index of these shows an indebtedness to the liberal arts of the Middle Ages (grammar, rhetoric, and logic) and the "more humane letters" of the Renaissance (philology [literature or poetry], history, and philosophy).[12] The liberal arts of the Middle Ages were universal methods that could be brought to bear upon any subject matter. A student became more human as he or she realized these general skills in interpretation, argument and disciplined creativity or scientific method. The more humane letters of the Renaissance humanized the students through a concentration upon the great works in literature and science, the great achievements of human beings. One became more human as he or she assimilated by taste and connaturality the poetry of Virgil or the mathematics of Euclid. For human beings become like what they learn to know and love.

Now I wonder if there is not a third state of the humanities, of the humanization of the student, coming somewhat incoherently into existence in Jesuit universities, thanks to the influence of the last two General Congregations and their concern for the justice that Christian faith necessarily includes. The insight is growing that one becomes more humane not simply because of the mastery of certain skills and the appreciation of human achievements, but by a disciplined growth in an awareness for and sensitivity to the hard life of the poor, the suffering of the exploited and the desperate—the lot of the vast majority of human beings. One becomes human as one feels the actual pain of the human race; one becomes less human as this pain is met with indifference and disinterest.

For the fact of the matter is that without such an educated and developed sensibility, the cultivation of the taste, imagination and intellect can result in an indifference that is all the more dehumanizing because of its isolation through self-congratulations. Dorothy Thompson was stunned to find the poetry of Goethe and the music of Beethoven in the SS barracks of Dachau. The irony cannot escape you when you remember that only ten years after Newman's great *Idea of a University* and its ideal product, the gentleman, Dostoevsky wrote in his *Notes from Underground* about the century of the Napoleonic wars and Irish starvation and the industrial ruin of hundreds of thousands: "Have you noticed that the most refined bloodletters were almost without exception the most civilized gentlemen? . . . because of civilization, man has become if not more bloodthirsty, then surely bloodthirsty in a worse, more repulsive way than before."[13]

Is it not *de facto* possible to have moved through a demanding course of liberal studies and in its resulting refinement to be almost complete unaware or indifferent to what is the life of the vast majority of human beings: the three to four million homeless in our cities, to be seen huddled at night over gratings during the winters; the migrant workers who are just about now beginning to follow the crops in California and the Midwest and who know that their children will have nothing better; the urban proletariat within our massive public housing projects, caught in a hopeless cycle of violence, drugs, unemployment, and terror—not to mention the disease, the unemployment, the hunger in the wretched lives of so many in the Third World? Let me be even more specific to this university. For any number of years, many wealthy families in Latin America sent their sons to Jesuit secondary schools and Jesuit colleges in the United States. When these men returned to their native countries, did they become part of the solution of the immense economic and social disparity among the people or did they become part of the problem? Was there any programmed effort in these Jesuit institutions to educate them in an awareness and a sensibility that would evoke a passion of social justice?

I would hope that this institute would deal with this issue of a developed sensibility, of a commitment to social justice, to human rights, to international responsibilities—not in a moralistic way, but as an essential part of the humanistic education of the student and of the life of the university. I am not speaking of propaganda, the kind of thing that has almost destroyed some universities as it became more frantic. I am speaking about the kinds of questions that Christian belief levels at a culture that is too limited. This conception of a more humane sensibility suggests the need for a radical development in our understanding of a precisely humanistic education, one which would result in a developed sensitivity, a set of questions, some serious study, and a knowledge that is profoundly humane. This development in humanistic education would come directly out of the conviction about a God to whom all human beings are dear and who, in the lovely words of the Leonine Sacramentary, "has wondrously established human nature and even more wonderfully established it anew."[14]

The task assigned to me was to contribute to an agenda for the Institute under consideration these days. I have recommended four problematic areas—all of them cognate with the traditions of the Society of Jesus and each of them intersecting with critical contemporary issues: the relationship between faith and intellectual culture; the kinds of questions and concerns that will define a contemporary university as Catholic; the architectonic, integrating character of theology and its relationship to the other disciplines; and an informed sensibility concerning human misery as a further development of the humanistic education of our students. There are obviously many more, but each of these embodies the theme to which we have set ourselves this afternoon.

Notes

1. See Michael J. Buckley, S.J., "Experience and Culture: A Point of Departure for American Atheism," *Theological Studies* 50:3 (1989) 443-65.

2. John Dewey, *A Common Faith* (New Haven: Yale University Press, 1968) 30.

3. E. C. Ladd and S. M. Lipset, *The Divided Academy* (New York: McGraw-Hill, 1975) 17.

4. *The Connecticut Mutual Life Report on American Values in the 80's: The Impact of Belief* (Hartford: Connecticut Mutual Life Insurance Company, 1981) 19.

5. *Gravissimum educationis* #8.

6. John Henry Cardinal Newman, *The Idea of a University*, Discourse ii (New York: Image, 1959) 61.

7. John Dewey, *Logic: The Theory of Inquiry* (New York: Holt, Rinehart and Winston, 1938) 108.

8. See Michael J. Buckley, S.J., "'*In Hunc Potissimum . .*': Ignatius' Understanding of a Jesuit University," *Readings in Ignatian Higher Education* (Washington, D.C.: Jesuit Conference, 1989) 18-27.

9. *Constitutions of the Society of Jesus* IV. 12, #447.

10. *Constitutions* IV. 12, #450.

11. See Michael Buckley, "The University and the Concern for Justice: The Search for a New Humanism," *Thought* 57:225 (1982) 219-233.

12. *Constitutions* IV. 12. #448.

13. Fyodor Dostoevsky, *Notes from Underground*, ed. Robert G. Durgy, trans. by Serge Skishkoff. The Crowell Critical Library (New York: Thomas Y. Crowell Company, 1969) 22-23.

14. This ancient prayer, which contains so profoundly the spirit of Christian humanism, *Deus qui humanae substantiae dignitatem,* is found initially as a Nativity Oration in the Leonine Sacramentary, a compilation dating from about 540 A.D. During the Carolingian period, it was transferred to the prayer over the water being mixed with wine. See Joseph A. Jungmann, S.J., *The Mass of the Roman Rite,* translated by Francis A. Brunner (New York: Benzinger Brothers, 1950) Vol. I, 62 and 94; Vol. II, 62ff.

Contributors

Michael J. Buckley, S.J., Professor of Systematic Theology at Notre Dame University, was for three years Executive Director of the Committee on Doctrine and the Committee on Pastoral Research and Practices of the U.S. National Conference of Catholic Bishops. Formerly professor of systematic theology at the Jesuit School of Theology at Berkeley, and widely known for his skill as a theological consultant, he is now increasingly hailed for his recently published magisterial study: *At the Origins of Modern Atheism* (Yale University Press, 1987). His paper suggests four ways in which various elements of the earlier Jesuit tradition, when hermeneutically transposed into contemporary culture, can help shape the agenda of a modern Jesuit university. Theology, for example, was understood in the *Constitutions* of Ignatius to be an architectonic discipline. However, it cannot function as architectonic except in vital contact with the arts and sciences. At the time of Ignatius and the early Jesuits, the medieval liberal arts were yielding to a renaissance model. Today the liberal arts are undergoing a further transposition which adds a new sense of their own nature and function. Humane development is seen to require a disciplined understanding and sensitivity to conditions of poverty, injustice and suffering. A modern university, as it attempts to inculate such a sensibility among its humanistic goals, may find itself developing new modes of being a university.

John Coleman, S.J., Professor of Religion and Society at the Jesuit School of Theology in Berkeley, is one of the leading theological theorists in the area of the sociology of religion. Already known to many at Boston College as a sometime visiting professor in the Institute of Religious Education of Pastoral Ministry, he is also a member of the editorial board of the journal *Concilium* (his most recent issue, October '89, was devoted to "Sport and Religion"), the

217

editor of a Paulist Press series on American Culture and Religion, and author of many articles and books, among them his acclaimed study: *American Strategic Theology* (1982). His paper will explore what has been happening to religious discourse as it gets caught between the cracks of the State and the Market, and how this affects the climate for belief in our culture.

Denis Donoghue, holder of the Henry James Chair of Letters at New York University, taught at University College, Dublin, and became a university lecturer and Fellow of King's College, Cambridge. He is one of the major contemporary critics of modern literature and culture. Prolific author of such works as *Connoisseurs of Chaos, The Ordinary Universe, Thieves of Fire, The Sovereign Ghost* and *Ferocious Alphabets,* and regular contributor to *The New York Times Book Review* and *The New York Review of Books,* Prof. Donoghue is already known at Boston College from several previous lecture visits. He is noted for his interest in the interconnection of religion and literature, a theme which pervades much of his writing and lecturing.

Jean Bethke Elshtain is the Centennial Professor of Political Science at Vanderbilt University. Her Brandeis dissertation was entitled: "Women and Politics: A Theoretical Analysis." She taught at the University of Massachusetts Amherst from 1973 to 1987, and has written or edited some half dozen books and dozens of articles dealing variously with the themes of man, woman, the family, power, war, politics, etc. Her 1981 Princeton University Press book: *Public Man, Private Woman: Woman in Social and Political Thought,* stands as one of her major achievements. Her paper explores the crisis in the American family by examining the paradox the family seems to represent for democratic culture. Neither a dictatorship nor a democracy, the family cannot be reduced to a contractual relationship, nor can it be replaced by anything else that will "do" what the family does, only do it more efficiently or, as some contend, more democratically. What, then, does the family do and what are those ethics, and their implications, that are constitutive of family relationships?

Rosemary Haughton, noted theologian and author, was raised in England where she married and became the mother of ten children and some foster children. She now lives in Gloucester, Massachusetts, as one of the founder-members of Wellspring House, a community committed to the provision of shelter for homeless families and to the development of innovative projects for low-income housing. She has written 36 books, among them: *The Catholic Thing* (1978), *The Passionate God* (1980), *The Re-Creation of Eve* (1985) and *Song in a Strange Land* (due Spring 1990). In looking ahead to her participation in the Inaugural Conference, she wrote: "Belief is not the same thing as faith. Belief struggles to give expression to the perceptions of reality which a person has acquired and has necessarily acquired from her or his cultural context. Faith is inarticulate and depends on the cultural experience for a voice and a vocabulary to give it form. But the faith experiences and daily perceptions of the individual, in his or her group, change more quickly than the available language of the culture and, therefore, always lack an entirely adequate language of belief. This is the perennial dilemma of the mystic, the heretic, the prophet, and the 'ordinary' believer, but it becomes acute to the point of schizophrenia in a culture as rapidly changing, as conflicted and as insecure as that of America in the nineteen-nineties."

Richard A. McCormick, S.J., the John A. O'Brien Professor of Christian Ethics at the University of Notre Dame, unchallenged patriarch of North American Catholic moral theologians, has published over a dozen books and hundreds of articles in more than a score of journals. His work deals with a whole range of Christian moral reflection and practice, and also delves courageously into theological and ecclesiological reflection. He is most known for his magisterial summaries of ethical scholarship which appeared for many years in *Theological Studies*, and for his contributions to bioethics and medical-moral problems. In his paper Father McCormick compares recent Vatican pronouncements on the "rights of the family" with the common English-tradition sense of rights. It investigates the striking similarity between, on the one hand, these Vatican-articulated rights and, on the other hand, some key principles applied by moral philosophers (e.g., in the bioethics text of T. Beauchamp and J. Childress) on the question of the rights of the protection of the person: (1) beneficence, (2) non-maleficence, (3) justice, (4) autonomy.

John W. O'Malley, S.J., Professor of Church History at the Weston School of Theology in Cambridge, was professor of history at the University of Detroit until 1979. He has written extensively on Renaissance and Reformation history, as well as on Roman Catholic developments in the age of modernity. His studies give him unusual insight into the spiritual, intellectual and cultural milieu in which the Society of Jesus was born and developed. Fr. O'Malley will begin his remarks on the task of the Jesuit Institute by analyzing the "estrangement between the arts and the Catholic Church" which Pope Paul VI acknowledged in 1964. He will try to show that this goes back, first to some shifts in the nature of theological culture that began in the thirteenth century and that had an impact much later, and, second, to some self-conscious decisions taken in the church about the place of art.

John W. Padberg, S.J., Director of the Institute of Jesuit Sources at St. Louis University, is known to many at Boston College from his service on the University's board of trustees from 1975 to 1983, and from his recently completed ten-year term as president of our Jesuit sister institution in Cambridge, the Weston School of Theology. Father Padberg, who has also served as Academic Dean at St. Louis University, is noted for a broad range of works dealing with the history of the Society of Jesus and with Jesuit life and spirituality. Known as one of the outstanding Jesuit teachers in North America, and for a dynamic lecturing style which simultaneously fascinates and provokes while also informing his hearers, Father Padberg attempts to "set the table" both for the Inaugural Conference and for the future work of the Jesuit Institute. His address outlines the context and explores the opportunities and challenges which face Boston College and its new research institute.

Anne E. Patrick, S.N.J.M., is currently President of the Catholic Theological Society of America and a resident scholar at the Institute for Ecumenical and Cultural Research, Collegeville, Minnesota. In September 1990 she will resume her post as Associate Professor and Chair of the Department of Religious at Carleton College in Northfield, Minnesota. She has published numerous articles on a broad range of theological, ethical, cultural and feminist issues, and she is now completing manuscripts entitled *Conscience and Community: Explorations in Catholic Moral Theology* and *Faith, Ethics, and Fiction: The Case of George Eliot's Last Novels.* She is also Director of the Society of Christian Ethics and an Editor for the Religious Book Club. In the chapter "On Not Running the Territorial Metaphor into the Ground: Toward a New Paradigm for Interdisciplinary Studies," she makes a case for theological contributions to literary discussions, argues for a conversational mode of interdisciplinary scholarship, and builds on Ignatian insights to suggest a research focus for the Jesuit Institute.

Preston N. Williams, Houghton Professor of Theology and Contemporary Change at Harvard Divinity School, is a contributing editor to *Christian Century* and author of numerous articles in a number of journals on issues dealing with the relationships between culture and ethics. He argues that while the family is a basic and fundamental unit in the society, the culture and normative ethic embedded in it exercises the dominant role in determining family structure and functioning. Using the American society and the African-American family as illustrations, Williams seeks to demonstrate how cultural values and institutions can and have acted to destroy healthy family life. In addition he suggests by references to Gunnar Myrdal and Daniel Patrick Moynihan how one can improve family life and meet the need for a just and good community by bringing into existence more adequate cultural norms and a family ethic suitable for the present period of rapidly changing family structure and function.